WordPerfect 6.1
for Windows

The Visual Learning Guide

Other Prima Visual Learning Guides

Word 6 for the Mac: The Visual Learning Guide

Cruising America Online

Quicken for Windows: The Visual Learning Guide

1-2-3 for Windows: The Visual Learning Guide

ACT! 2.0 for Windows: The Visual Learning Guide

Excel for the Mac: The Visual Learning Guide

Windows 3.1: The Visual Learning Guide

Excel 5 for Windows: The Visual Learning Guide

PowerPoint: The Visual Learning Guide

Word for Windows 6: The Visual Learning Guide

WordPerfect 6 for Windows: The Visual Learning Guide

WinFax PRO: The Visual Learning Guide

Upcoming Books!

WinComm PRO: The Visual Learning Guide

PROCOMM PLUS for Windows: The Visual Learning Guide

Windows 95: The Visual Learning Guide

How to Order:

Individual orders and quantity discounts are available from the publisher, Prima Publishing, P.O. Box 1260BK, Rocklin, CA 95677-1260; (916) 632-4400. For quantity orders, include information on your letterhead concerning the intended use of the books and the number of books you wish to purchase.

WordPerfect 6.1 for Windows

The Visual Learning Guide

Grace Joely Beatty, Ph.D.

David C. Gardner, Ph.D.

PRIMA PUBLISHING

Project Editor: Susan Silva

WordPerfect 6.1™ is a registered trademark of Microsoft Corporation.

If you have a problem installing or running WordPerfect 6.1, notify WordPerfect Corporation at (800) 321-5906. Prima Publishing cannot provide software support.

ISBN: 1-7615-0091-X
Library of Congress Card Number: 95-68597
95 96 97 98 AA 10 9 8 7 6 5 4 3 2 1
Printed in the United States of America

Acknowledgments

We are deeply indebted to reviewers around the country who gave generously of their time to test every step in the manuscript. Ray Bumgardner, David Coburn, Carolyn Holder, and Tina Terhark cannot be thanked enough!

Linda Beatty worked with us to write chapters and is now the Spell Check champion of the world. Thanks to Linda Miles for her technical edits.

We are personally and professionally delighted to work with everyone at Prima Publishing.

Bill Gladstone and Matt Wagner of Waterside Productions created the idea for this series. Their faith in us has never wavered.

Joseph and Shirley Beatty made this series possible. We can never repay them.

Asher Schapiro has always been there when we needed him.

Paula Gardner Capaldo and David Capaldo have been terrific. Thanks, Joshua and Jessica, for being wonderful kids. Our project humorist, Mike Bumgardner, always came through when we needed a boost!

We could not have made the deadlines without the technical support of Ray Holder, our electrical genius; Diana M. Balelo, Frank E. Straw, Daniel W. Terhark, Martin J. O'Keefe of Computer Service & Maintenance, our computer wizards.

Contents

Customize
Your Learning

Prima Visual Learning Guides are not like any other computer books you have ever seen. They are based on our years in the classroom, our corporate consulting, and our research at Boston University on the best ways to teach technical information to non-technical learners. Most importantly, this series is based on the feedback of a panel of reviewers from across the country who range in computer knowledge from "panicked at the thought" to sophisticated.

This is not an everything-you've-ever-wanted-to-know-about-WordPerfect 6.1 book. It is designed to give you the information you need to perfom all of the basic (and many advanced) functions with confidence and skill. It is a book that our reviewers claim makes it "really easy" for anyone to learn WordPerfect 6.1 quickly.

Each chapter is illustrated with actual screens to guide you through every task. The combination of screens, step-by-step instructions, and pointers make it impossible for you to get lost or confused as you follow along on your own computer. You can either work through from beginning to end or skip around to master the skills you need.

We truly hope you'll like using this book and the WordPerfect 6.1 program. Let us know how you feel about our book and whether there are any changes or improvements we can make. You can contact us through Prima Publishing or send us an e-mail letter. Our Internet address is Write.Bks@aol.com. Thanks for buying the book. Enjoy!

Joely and David

Changing Margins and Fonts and Entering Text

If you've never used WordPerfect for Windows, you are in for a treat. If you are upgrading to version 6.1, you will love the exciting new features. In this chapter, you will do the following:

- ✓ Open a WordPerfect document
- ✓ Set margins
- ✓ Change the font for the current document
- ✓ Change the font for all future documents
- ✓ Enter text
- ✓ Use special fonts to insert symbols into the text

OPENING WORDPERFECT FOR THE FIRST TIME

1. **Type win** at the **c:\>** (C prompt) on your screen to open, or boot up, Windows. You will probably have different group icons at the bottom of your screen than you see in this example.

2. **Click twice** quickly on the **WPWin 6.1** group icon or the group icon that contains WordPerfect. It will open up to a group window that contains a number of icons. It's okay if your group window is in a different shape or position than the one you see in the next example.

```
┌─────────────────────────────────────────────────────┐
│ ═                    Program Manager            ▼│▲│
│ File   Options   Window   Help                       │
│                                                      │
│                                                      │
│                                                      │
│                                                      │
│                                                      │
│                                                      │
│                                                      │
│                                                      │
│  ▦      ▦       ▦       ▦                            │
│ America Online PROCOMM Adaptec SCSI  WPWin 6.1       │
│         PLUS 2.0                                      │
│                                                      │
│  ▦      ▦      ▦       ▦      ▦     ▦     ▦     ▦   │
│ LANtastic Games  Main  Accessories Corel 4 On-Line StartUp GBGroup │
└─────────────────────────────────────────────────────┘
```

3. **Click twice** on the **WordPerfect** icon. You will see an hourglass, then the copyright information for WordPerfect. Then, after a brief time, you will see the opening WordPerfect screen with the dialog box shown below.

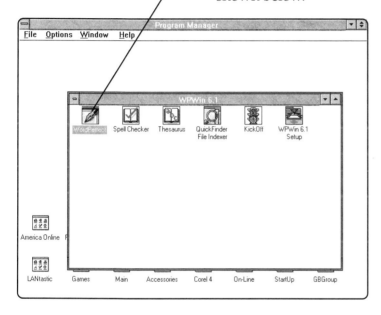

4. **Click** on **No**. The dialog box will disappear.

You can still see QuickStart Coach at any time by clicking on the Coach button in the toolbar, then clicking on QuickStart.

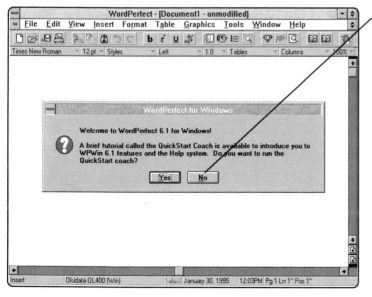

Notice that the Title bar says "WordPerfect - [Document1-unmodified]." This will change when you name the document in Chapter 2, "Naming and Saving a Document."

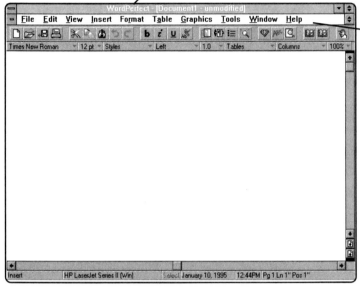

The Menu bar is under the title bar.

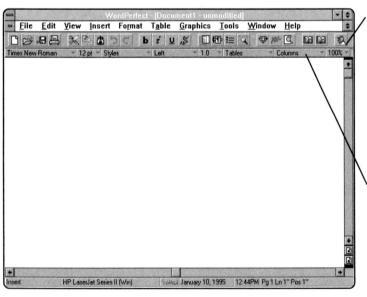

The Toolbar contains icons, or pictures, that represent common tasks like printing a file, adding an image, and checking the spelling in your document. You will learn how to use these features later in the book.

The Power Bar gives you quick access to other features, such as Font Face, Font Size, and Style.

SETTING MARGINS

The standard (default) margins in WordPerfect are preset at 1 inch for the top, bottom, left, and right margins. You can change any or all of these settings as many times as you want within a document. Each time you make a change, the new margin applies in the document until you change it again. In this example you will change the top margin.

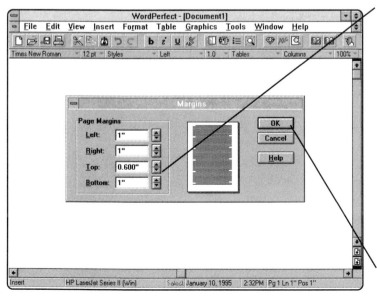

1. **Click** on **Format** in the menu bar. A pull-down menu will appear.

2. **Click** on **Margins**. The Margins dialog box will appear.

3. **Click four times** on the ▼ to the right of the Top Margin box. The 1" will change to 0.600". You're making the top margin smaller to give yourself the extra room to create a letterhead in Chapter 7. (If you are going to print on stationery that already has a letterhead, the top margin for a short-to-medium-length letter should be about 2.5 inches.)

4. **Click** on **OK**. The Margins dialog box will close.

CHANGING THE FONT

When you change the font in a document on your screen, it affects only that document. However, you can also change the default, or initial, font so that all future documents are affected.

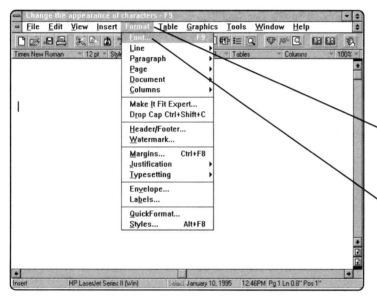

Changing the Font for the Current Document

1. **Click** on **Format** in the menu bar. A pull-down menu will appear.

2. **Click** on **Font**. The Font dialog box will appear.

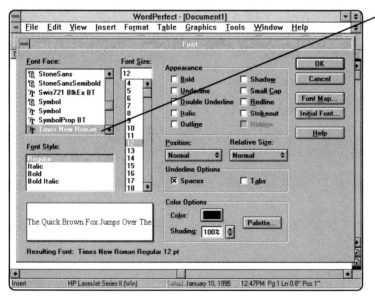

The font that is highlighted when this dialog box opens is determined by your printer and the fonts you have installed. In this example, Times New Roman is highlighted.

3. **Type** the letter **a**. This will move the highlight bar in the Font Face box up to the first font beginning with the letter a.

4. **Click** on **Arial** if it is not already highlighted. (Arial may not be the first font in your list.)

Notice that 12 is already in the Font Size box. Because business correspondence is usually typed in a 10- or 12-point type, leave the font size at 12.

Notice the sample of the selected font in the Resulting Font box. Use the ↓ key on your keyboard to move through the list of fonts and watch the sample font change. However, if you want your screen to look like the examples in the book, make sure you go back to Arial.

Continue on to the next section to change the font for page numbers, headers, footers, and notes.

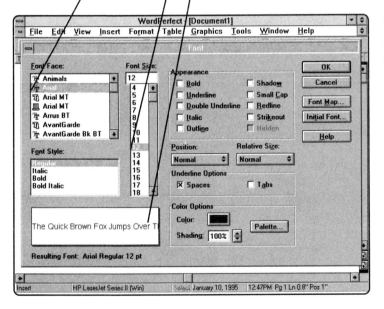

CHANGING THE FONT FOR PAGE NUMBERS, HEADERS, FOOTERS, AND NOTES

The font for page numbers, headers, footers, and notes is controlled by a different dialog box than the Font dialog box, which controls the text in the letter. In this example you will change this font to Arial to match the font for the body of the document.

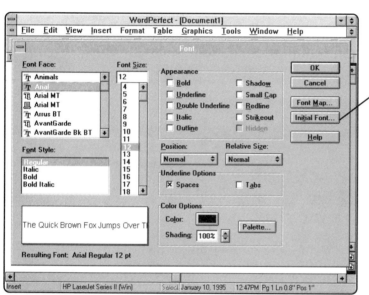

1. **Click** on **Initial Font** in the Font dialog box. The Document Initial Font dialog box will appear. (If you have not been following along with this chapter, go back to the previous section, "Changing the Font," to open the Font dialog box.)

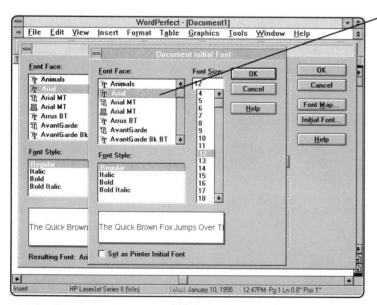

2. **Type** the letter **a** to move the highlight bar to the top of the Font Face list if the highlight bar is not already there.

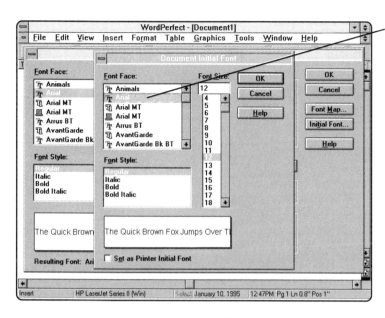

3. **Click** on **Arial** if it is not already highlighted.

4. **Leave** the **Font Size** at **12**.

You can change the font for all future documents to Arial in this dialog box. So instead of clicking on OK to close the dialog box, go on to the following section to change the Initial Font.

CHANGING THE FONT FOR FUTURE DOCUMENTS

If you have not been following along with this chapter, go back and follow the steps under "Changing the Font" to open the Font dialog box and then the Document Initial Font dialog box.

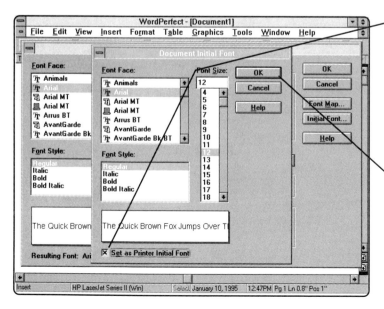

1. **Click** on **Set as Printer Initial Font** to insert an X in the box. This tells WordPerfect to change the font that will appear in all future documents to Arial 12 point type.

2. **Click** on **OK**. The Document Initial Font dialog box will disappear. The Font dialog box will still be on your screen.

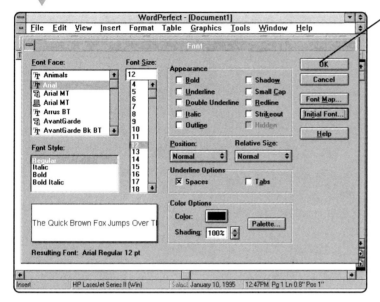

3. **Click** on **OK** to close the Font dialog box.

ENTERING TEXT

You are now ready to type a letter. In the following examples you will type a letter from Dragon Costume Designs, inviting a customer to the Annual Costume Preview.

Creating the Letterhead

The insertion point will be flashing at the beginning of the document. This means you can start typing, and the text will begin at this point. The first thing you will type is the company name and return address.

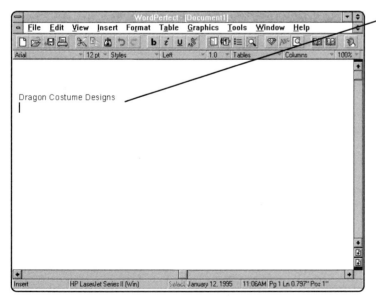

1. **Type Dragon Costume Designs**. If you make a typing error, simply press the Backspace key on your keyboard as many times as necessary to erase the wrong letters. Type the correct letters.

2. **Press Enter.** The insertion point will move to the next line.

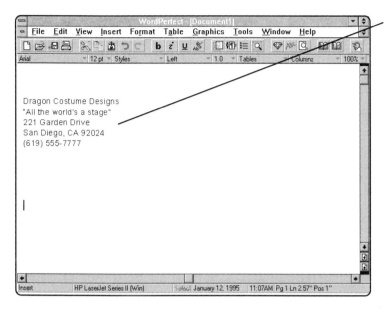

3. Type "**All the world's a stage**" and **press Enter**.

4. Type **221 Garden Drive** and **press Enter**.

5. Type **San Diego, CA 92024**. (**Press** the **Spacebar twice** after CA.) **Press Enter**.

6. Type **(619) 555-7777**.

7. **Press Enter six times**.

Entering the Date, Address, and Salutation

1. **Click** on **Insert** in the menu bar. A pull-down menu will appear.

2. **Click** on **Date**. A second menu will appear.

3. **Click** on **Date Text**. The dialog box will close.

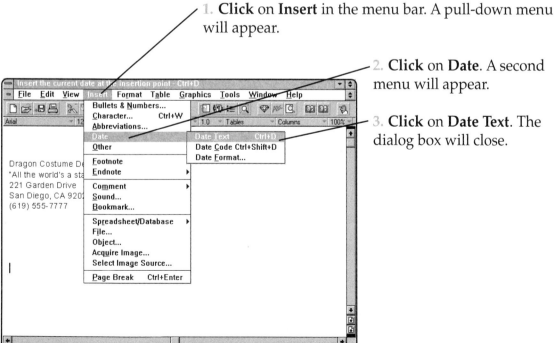

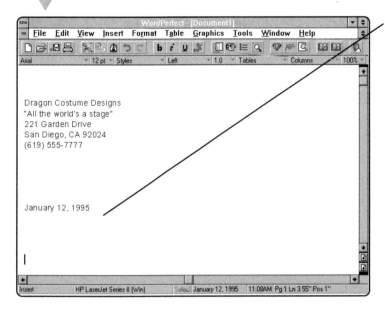

Notice that today's date has been inserted in your document.

4. **Press Enter five times**.

5. **Type** the following lines (**press Enter** after each line):

Ms. Diane Hendersen
Holder Dance Company
1720 Raymon Way
Santa Barbara, CA 12345

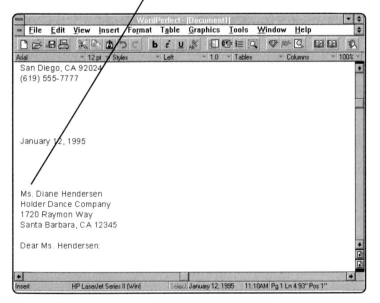

(Be sure to **press** the **Spacebar twice** after CA.)

6. **Press Enter twice** after the last line.

7. **Type Dear Ms. Hendersen:** (don't forget the colon).

8. **Press Enter twice**. The screen will automatically scroll (move up) to make room for the additional lines.

Entering the Body of the Letter

You are now ready to enter the body of the letter. Like all word-processing programs, you can type without worrying about your right margin. WordPerfect will wrap the text around to the next line automatically.

There is another way in which word processing is different from typing. On the typewriter you press the spacebar twice after a period at the end of a sentence. In word processing you press the spacebar only *once* after the period at the end of a sentence.

1. **Type** the text below. It contains errors (shown in italics) that you will correct later, so include them if you want to follow along with these procedures. If you make an unintentional typing error, press the Backspace key and type the correct letters. Press Enter twice to create a new paragraph.

We hope you will be *her* at our Annual Costume Preview on Thursday, March 3, at 2 p.m. (Remember to press Enter twice at the end of this sentence to begin a new paragraph.)

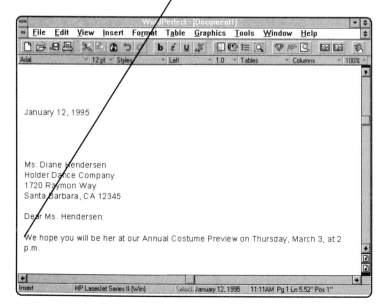

Note: As you type the body of the letter, you may notice minor differences in the point at which words move to the next line. It's perfectly alright to have slight differences. Just be aware that the differences are because your printer and driver are probably different from the ones we use and not because of any mistake on your part. (We are using a LaserJet II with a WordPerfect driver.)

2. **Type** the following paragraphs. **Press Enter twice after each paragraph** to insert a double space.

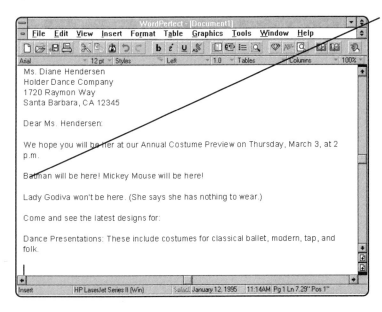

Batman will be here! Mickey Mouse will be here!

Lady Godiva won't be here. (She says she has nothing to wear.)

Come and see the latest designs for:

Dance Presentations: These include costumes for classical ballet, modern, tap, and folk.

Theatrical Presentations: These include costumes for performances such as Cats, Les Miserables, and Phantom of the Opera.

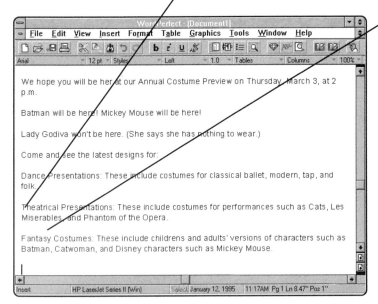

Fantasy Costumes: These include *childrens* and adults' versions of characters such as Batman, Catwoman, and Disney characters such as Mickey Mouse. (Remember to **press Enter twice** to start the next paragraph.)

3. **Type** the following paragraphs. **Press Enter twice after each paragraph** to insert a double space.

Historical Figures: These include costumes for figures such as Napoleon and Josephine and masks for current political figures.

Because you are a valued customer, Ms. Hendersen, you will *recieve* a 20 percent discount on any order placed at the Preview.

Please return a copy of the reply form below by Wednesday, February 23.

(Remember to **Press Enter twice** after the last line.)

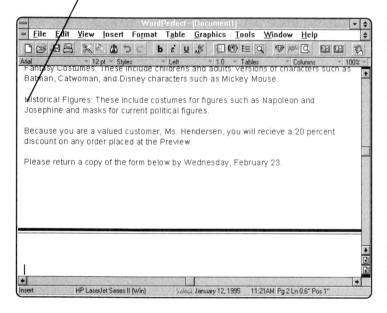

Notice that you have moved to a new page on the screen. This is the *automatic page break*. You will learn how to change the location of the page break in Chapter 6, "Editing a Document."

The exact location of the automatic page break depends on the margins you set and the size of the font you use. It also depends on the printer and printer driver you select.

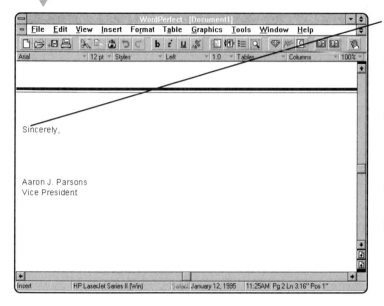

4. **Type Sincerely,**

5. **Press Enter five times**.

6. **Type Aaron J. Parsons** and **press Enter**.

7. **Type Vice President**.

8. **Press Enter seven times**. Your screen will look like this example.

INSERTING SYMBOLS AND FINISHING THE LETTER

WordPerfect 6.1 for Windows comes with a variety of character sets that range from symbols to foreign language alphabets. In this section, you will insert two different symbols into the text.

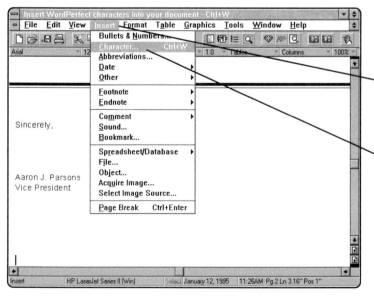

Inserting a Scissors Symbol

1. **Click** on **Insert** in the menu bar. A pull-down menu will appear.

2. **Click** on **Character**. The WordPerfect Characters dialog box will appear.

Notice that Iconic Symbols is selected.

3. **Click three times** on the ⬇ on the scroll bar in the dialog box so that you can see the scissors.

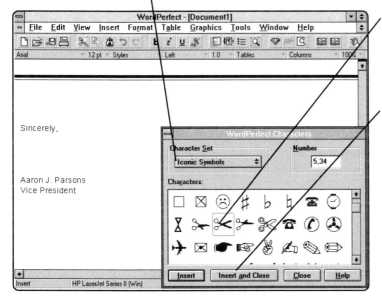

4. **Click** on the second **Scissors** symbol. A dotted box will appear around the scissors.

5. **Click** on **Insert and Close**. The dialog box will disappear, and a pair of scissors will be inserted into your text.

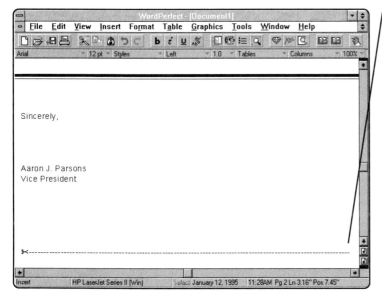

6. **Press and hold** the **hyphen key** on your keyboard to type a dotted line across the page. If you go too far and the hyphens start showing on the second line, simply press the Backspace key until the cursor is at the end of the first line of hyphens.

7. **Press** the **Enter key twice** to insert a double space after the hyphens.

Inserting Box Symbols

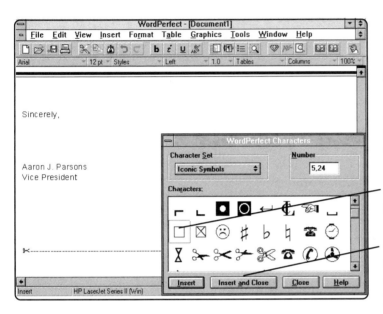

1. Repeat steps 1 and 2 in the previous section to open the WordPerfect Characters dialog box.

2. Click on the ⬆ on the scroll bar, if necessary, so that you can see the square.

3. Click on the **square** symbol.

4. Click on **Insert and Close**. The square symbol will be inserted into the letter.

5. Press the **Spacebar**. Then **type** the sentence **I will be attending.** Then **press Enter twice**.

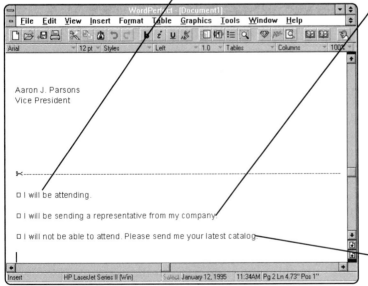

6. Repeat steps 1 through 4 to insert another square into the text.

7. Type the sentence **I will be sending a representative from my company.** Then **press Enter twice**.

8. Repeat steps 1 through 4 to insert the square into the text a third time.

9. Type the following sentences: **I will not be able to attend. Please send me your latest catalog.** Then **press Enter twice**.

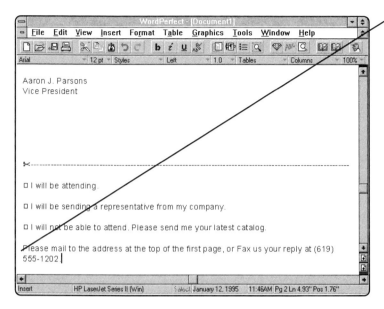

10. **Type** the sentence **Please mail to the address at the top of the first page, or Fax us your reply at (619) 555-1202.**

Congratulations! You just created a letter in WordPerfect. In Chapter 2, you will name the letter and save it.

Naming and Saving a Document

Saving a document or file in WordPerfect is as easy as clicking your mouse. WordPerfect is set up to save files to the WPDOCS directory, which is a subdirectory of WPWIN. In this chapter, you will do the following:

✔ Name and save a document

NAMING AND SAVING A FILE

In this section you will name the letter you typed in Chapter 1 and save it to the WPDOCS directory.

1. **Click** on the **Save button** in the toolbar. Because you have not named the file, the Save As dialog box will appear.

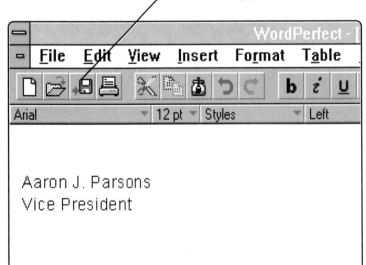

Notice that this is a magnified view of the upper-left corner of your screen. You will see both regular views and magnified views in this book.

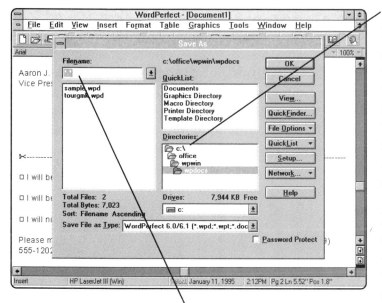

Notice the open folders beside c:\, office, wpwin, and wpdocs. These tell you that you are currently working in wpdocs, which is a subdirectory of wpwin, which is a subdirectory of office. The wpdocs, wpwin, and office directories are all on the C drive.

If you installed WordPerfect 6.1 over a previous version of WordPerfect, the 6.1 version will pick up the settings you had in the previous version, and this dialog box may look a little different from what you see here.

Because the cursor is already flashing in the Filename box and the correct folders are open, you can simply go to step 2 and type a name for your file. Filenames can have no more than eight characters with no spaces.

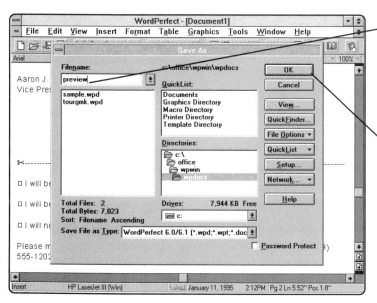

2. **Type preview**. WordPerfect will automatically add the .wpd extension (for WordPerfect document) when it saves the file.

3. **Click** on **OK**. Your file is now saved.

Notice that the document is now named
preview.wpd-unmodified.

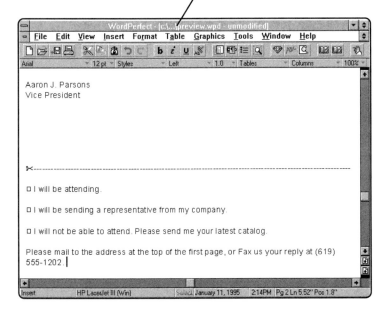

Once you have named a
file, clicking on the Save
button will not bring up the
Save As dialog box. It will
simply save any changes
you have made to your file.
As you work on a file, use
the Save button often.

Printing a Document

In WordPerfect 6.1 for Windows, you can print the whole document, the current page, or selected pages. You can click on the Print button in the toolbar or you can use the File pull-down menu. Both methods will bring up the Print dialog box. In this chapter, you will do the following:

✓ Print all or part of a document using the Print button
✓ Print all or part of a document using the File pull-down menu

PRINTING A DOCUMENT WITH THE PRINT BUTTON

In this section you will use the Print button in the toolbar to print a document. The Preview file should be open if you've been following along with this book. Also, make sure your printer is turned on or you will get an error message when you try to print.

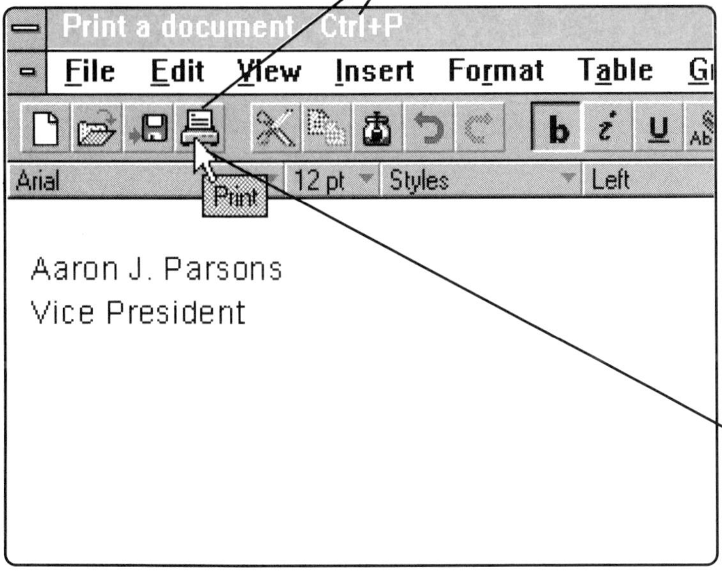

1. **Place** the **mouse pointer** on top of the **Print button**. Notice that the button's function appears in a balloon and in the title bar. The title bar also shows you a keystroke combination that will do the same thing as the button. If you press and hold the Ctrl key and press the letter p (Ctrl + p), you can print a document without using the mouse.

Print a document   Ctrl+P

| File | Edit | View | Insert | Format | Table | G |

Arial   12 pt ▾ Styles   ▾ Left

Print

Aaron J. Parsons
Vice President

2. **Click** on the **Print button** in the toolbar. The Print dialog box will appear.

Printing the Current Page

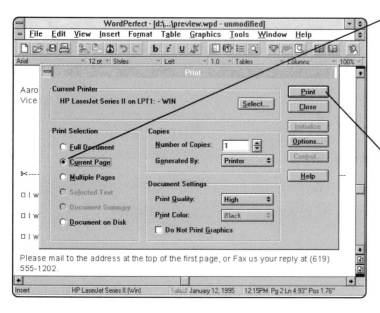

1. **Click** on **Current Page** to insert a dot in the circle. This instructs WordPerfect to print only the page where your cursor is located.

2. **Click** on **Print**. After a pause, a message box will appear briefly. The current page will print, and the dialog box will close.

Printing Selected Pages

1. **Click** on the **Print button** in the menu bar. The Print dialog box will appear as you see here.

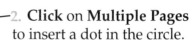

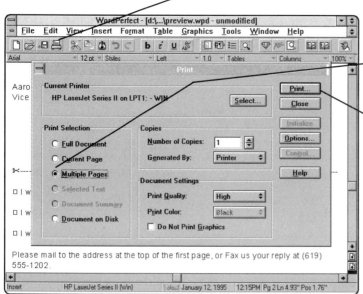

2. **Click** on **Multiple Pages** to insert a dot in the circle.

3. **Click** on **Print**. The Multiple Pages dialog box will appear.

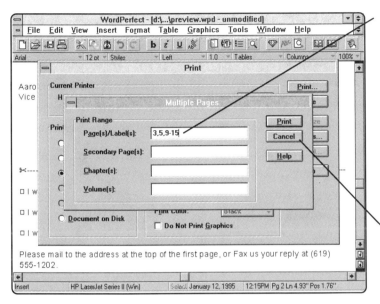

4. **Type 3,5,9-15**. It will replace the highlighted "all." This specifies that pages 3, 5, and 9 through 15 are to be printed. Since this document isn't that long, cancel out of this dialog box. If the document were that long, you would simply click on Print.

5. **Click** on **Cancel**. The Print dialog box will reappear.

Printing the Entire Document

1. **Click** on **Full Document** to insert a dot in the circle.

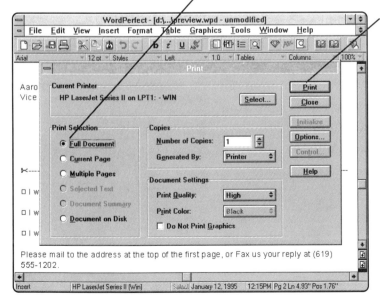

2. **Click** on **Print**. You will see a message box saying "Preparing document for printing." Then the entire document will print.

PRINTING A DOCUMENT WITH THE FILE PULL-DOWN MENU

Using the File pull-down menu will also bring up the Print dialog box.

1. **Click** on **File** in the menu bar. A pull-down menu will appear.

2. **Click** on **Print**. The Print dialog box will appear. Refer to the steps shown earlier in the chapter to print the current page, selected pages, or the entire document.

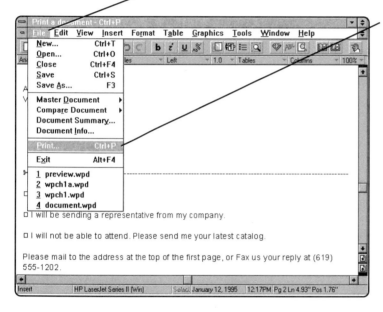

Closing a File and Opening a Saved File

Since WordPerfect 6.1 is a Windows-based program, it uses standard Windows commands to open and close files. As in all Windows programs, there are several ways to open and close files. In this chapter, you will do the following:

✓ Close a file
✓ Close WordPerfect for Windows
✓ Learn two ways to open a saved file

CLOSING A FILE

In this section you will close the preview.wpd file you created in Chapter 1. Since WordPerfect will prompt you to save if you have made any changes since your last save, there is no need to worry about losing changes to your file.

1. **Click** on **File** in the menu bar. A pull-down menu will appear.

2. **Click** on **Close**.

If you haven't made any changes to preview.wpd since you saved in Chapter 2, WordPerfect will simply close the file, and a blank WordPerfect screen will appear.

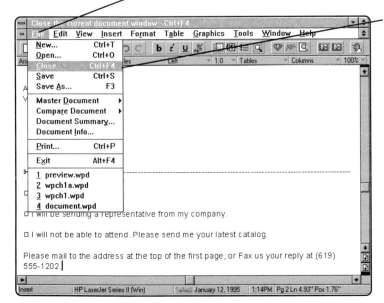

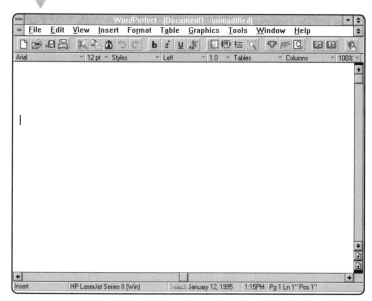

Your screen will look like the example to the left.

Closing After Changes

Note: If you have been following along with the previous chapters, you won't see the screen in the following example because you saved your document before you closed it.

If, however, you have made changes since the last time you saved, you will see the following screen when you try to close the file.

a. **Click** on **Yes** to save the changes to the file.

or

b. **Click** on **No** to close without saving the changes.

or

c. **Click** on **Cancel** to cancel the close command.

CLOSING WORDPERFECT FOR WINDOWS

In this section you will close the WordPerfect program.

1. **Click twice** on the **Control menu box** (▢) on the left of the WordPerfect title bar. After a pause WordPerfect will close, and you will be back at Program Manager with the group that contains the WordPerfect icon.

BOOTING UP WORDPERFECT

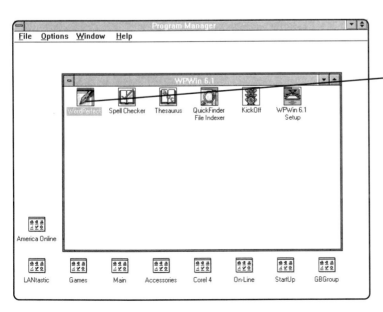

"Boot up" is computer talk for start.

1. **Click twice** on the **WordPerfect icon** in whatever group it happens to be.

After a pause, WordPerfect will appear on your screen with a blank Document1 file.

OPENING A SAVED FILE

There are several ways to open a saved file. In Method #1, you will use the File pull-down menu.

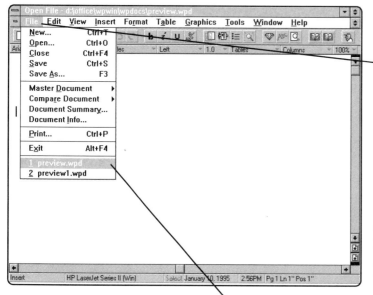

Method #1

1. **Click** on **File** in the menu bar. A pull-down menu will appear.

At the bottom of the File pull-down menu you will see up to four files listed depending on whether you have a new WordPerfect program or others have used WordPerfect before you.

2. **Click** on **preview.wpd** in the file list. The file will appear on your screen.

Method #2

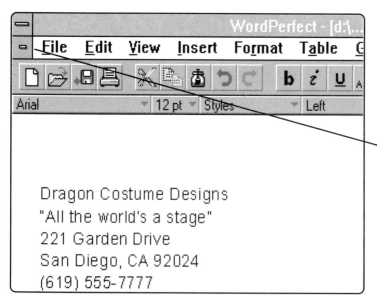

Method #2 uses the Open button in the toolbar. To try this method, you will have to close the preview.wpd file.

1. **Click twice** on the **Control menu box** (⊟) to the left of the menu bar to close the file. (Be careful not to click on the Control menu box in the WordPerfect title bar. That will close the entire program.)

2. **Click** on the **Open button** in the toolbar. The Open File dialog box will appear.

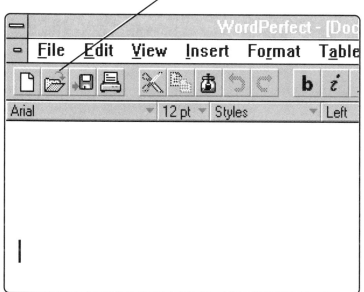

Notice that the wpdocs directory appears in the directories list box.

3. **Click twice** on **preview.wpd** in the File Name list box. The file will appear on your screen. If others have used WordPerfect, you may have other files listed in this box. (You can also click once on preview.wpd to highlight it, then click on OK.)

In the next chapter you will learn how to use the Grammar and Spelling Checker and the Thesaurus that comes with WordPerfect.

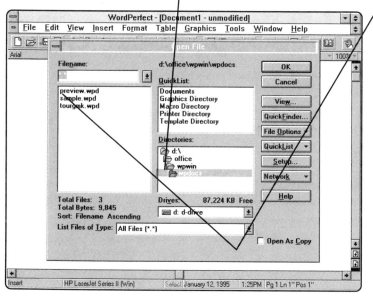

CHAPTER

5

Checking Grammar and Spelling, and Using the Thesaurus

WordPerfect has two handy utilities that will check your spelling and grammar and make suggestions for changes. It also contains a Thesaurus that will offer a list of synonyms and antonyms. Now, if it would only go out for coffee . . .

In this chapter, you will do the following:

✓ Use Grammatik to check the grammar and spelling
✓ Use the Thesaurus

CHOOSING A CHECKER

WordPerfect contains both a spelling checker and a grammar checker.

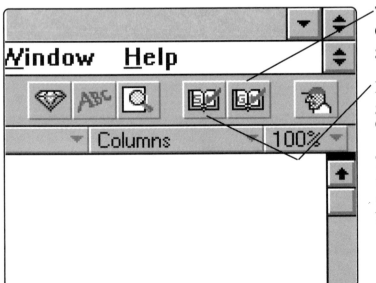

The grammar checker, Grammatik, checks both grammar and spelling.

If you don't want to check grammar, use the Spelling Checker.

The examples in this chapter will show the grammar checker so you can see how both functions work.

CHECKING GRAMMAR
AND SPELLING

WordPerfect is set up to automatically go to the beginning of a document when you start Grammatik, so it doesn't matter where the cursor is when you begin this process. This section, however, does show the cursor at the beginning of the letter.

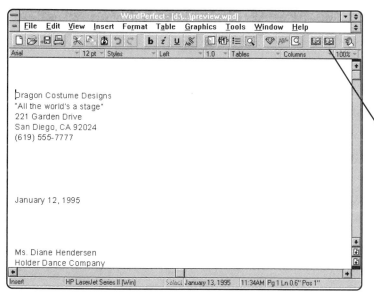

1. **Click** on the **Grammatik button** on the right of the toolbar. The Grammatik dialog box will appear. (You can also click on Tools in the menu bar, then click on Grammatik.)

In this example, Grammatik has identified world's as a possessive noun. However, because world's is correctly used here as a contraction and as a direct quote, ignore the suggestion.

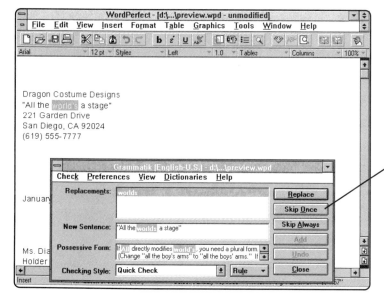

2. **Click** on **Skip Once**. This will cause the Grammatik to skip the word once but highlight the word the next time it appears in the document. Grammatik will then identify the next error.

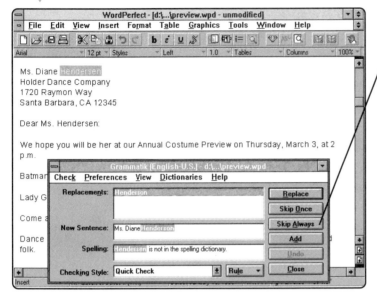

Next, Hendersen is identified as a misspelled word.

3. Click on **Skip Always**. This will skip every occurrence of Hendersen in the letter. Grammatik will next identify Ramon as a misspelled word.

4. Click on **Skip Once** to skip Ramon.

Next, Grammatik has identified the 2 in 2 p.m. as an error and says that before p.m., time should be written out completely.

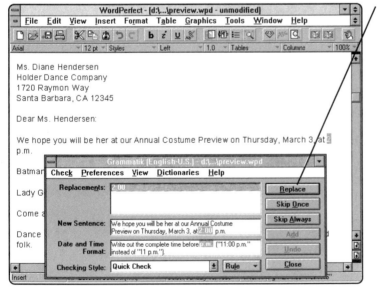

5. Click on **Replace**. Grammatik will insert the correct text and identify the next error.

Grammatik has identified "her" as an error, but for the wrong reason. This is another example of why computers are not ready to rule the world. In this example the suggested replacement is not appropriate so you will have to edit the word directly in the document.

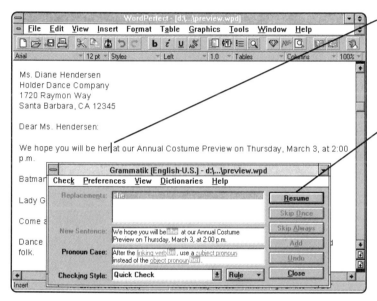

6. **Click** to the **right** of **her** in the letter.

7. **Type** the letter **e** to change the word to here.

8. **Click** on **Resume**. Grammatik will highlight the next error.

9. **Click** on **Skip Once** when Grammatik identifies each of the following words as misspelled: Godiva
                                         Miserables

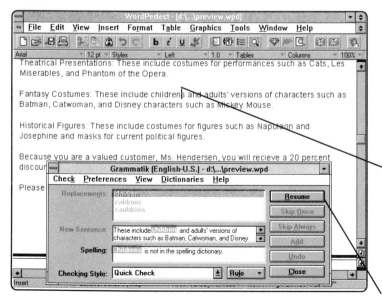

Grammatik has identified childrens as a misspelled word but the suggestions do not include a plural possessive form. However, you can correct the word in the letter.

10. **Click between n** and **s** to place the cursor.

11. **Type '** (an apostrophe) to change the word to children's.

12. **Click** on **Resume**.

Adding a Word to the Dictionary

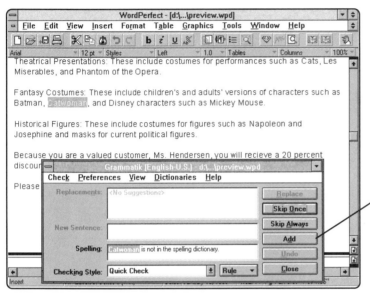

WordPerfect uses a standard dictionary to check words. If you use a nonstandard word frequently (such as a proper name), you can add it to the dictionary. In this example you will add Catwoman to the Document Dictionary.

1. **Click** on **Add**. Catwoman is now added to the Document Dictionary.

Grammatik will go on to highlight the next possible error.

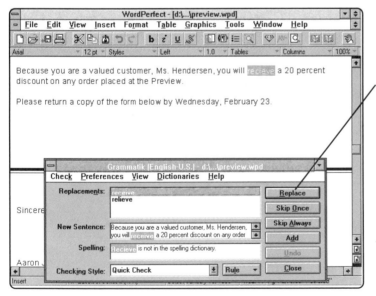

In this example, Grammatik has identified "recieve" as a misspelled word.

2. Because the correct word, receive, is highlighted in the suggestions list, **click** on **Replace**. The misspelled word will be replaced by the correct word.

Completing the Check

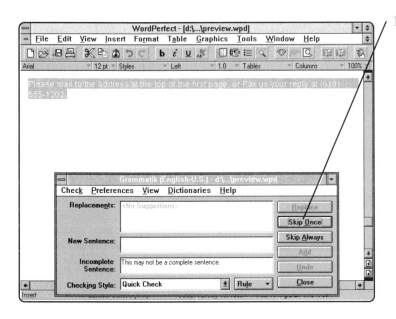

1. **Click** on **Skip Once**.

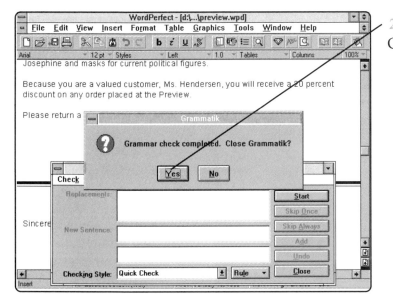

2. **Click** on **Yes** to close Grammatik.

USING THE THESAURUS

In this section you will use the Thesaurus to view words that can replace "latest." First, however, you will use the Search feature to locate "latest."

Using Find and Replace

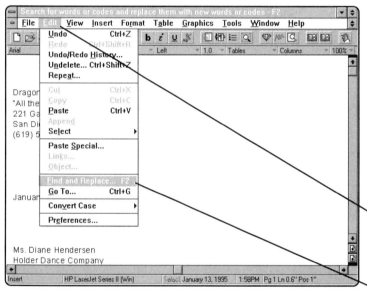

You can search forward or backward in a document. In this example you will go to the beginning of the file and search from that point.

1. **Press and hold** the **Ctrl key** then **press** the **Home key** (Ctrl + Home) to go to the top of the file.

2. **Click** on **Edit** in the menu bar. A pull-down menu will appear.

3. **Click** on **Find and Replace**. The Find and Replace Text dialog box will appear.

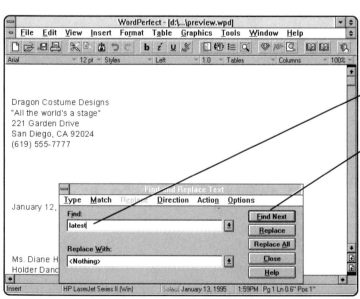

4. **Type latest** in the Find box.

5. **Click** on **Find Next** to go to the next time the word "latest" appears after the cursor position.

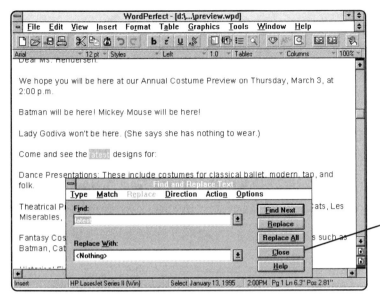

Notice that the first occurrence of latest is highlighted in the letter. Because this is the word you want to change, close the dialog box. (If you wanted another occurrence of latest, you would click on Find Next again until the one you wanted was highlighted.)

6. **Click** on **Close** to close the dialog box.

Opening the Thesaurus

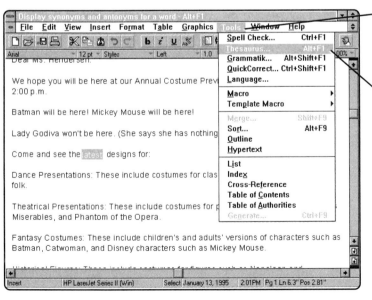

1. **Click** on **Tools** in the menu bar. A pull-down menu will appear.

2. **Click** on **Thesaurus**. The Thesaurus dialog box will appear.

3. **Click** on the ⬇ on the scroll bar to scroll through the various choices.

As you scroll through the list, notice that there are three sections in the list:

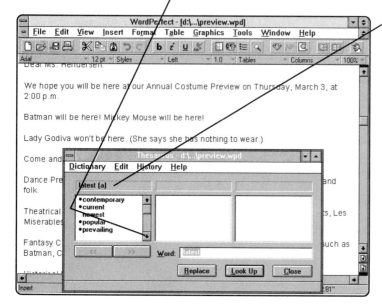

The first section shows synonyms (similar words) for latest as an adjective under the heading "latest [a]" as you see in this example.

The second section shows synonyms for latest as a noun under the heading "latest [n]."

The third section shows antonyms (opposites) under the heading "latest [ant]."

4. **Click** on ⬆ on the scroll bar to go back to the top of the list.

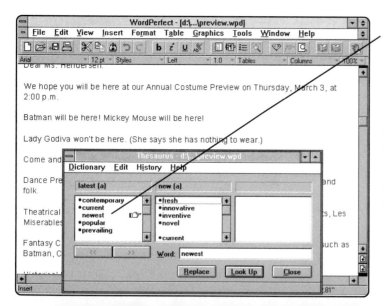

5. **Click twice** on **newest**. A second list will appear with synonyms and antonyms for newest.

If you click twice on a word in the second list, such as "fresh," a third list will appear with synonyms and antonyms for fresh.

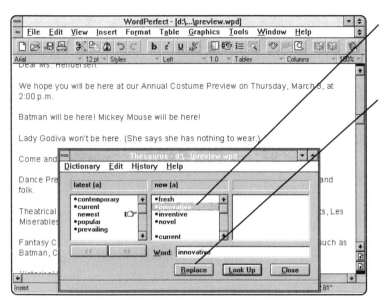

6. **Click** on **innovative** in the second list. It will be highlighted.

7. **Click** on **Replace**. The dialog box will disappear and innovative will replace latest in the letter.

SAVING YOUR WORK

1. **Click** on **File** in the menu bar. A pull-down menu will appear.

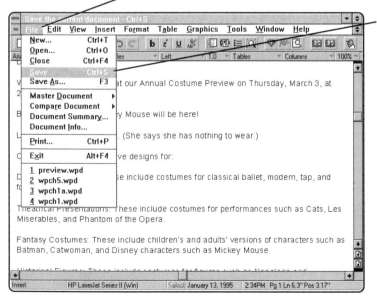

2. **Click** on **Save** to save your work. You can, of course, click on the Save button on the toolbar instead of using the File pull-down menu. You can also press and hold the Ctrl key then type s (Ctrl + s) to save.

Editing a Document

WordPerfect 6.1 has a number of nifty editing features. Using the mouse and scroll bars makes moving through your document easy. Highlighting text allows you to delete, move, and copy with ease. You'll love the new drag-and-drop moving and copying features. You can even use an Edit Undo when you change your mind. In this chapter, you will do the following:

✓ Show paragraph formatting marks
✓ Add and delete letters and words and combine paragraphs
✓ Use the Edit Undo feature
✓ Use the Replace All command to correct an error that occurs in several places
✓ Move, copy, and paste text
✓ Insert and change the position of the page break

INSERTING TEXT

In this section you will display paragraph symbols and add text to a paragraph. You will also learn to move around in your document.

Moving in a Document

1. Press and hold the **Ctrl key** and **press** the **Home key** (Ctrl + Home). This will place the cursor at the beginning of the file as you see in this example.

Displaying Paragraph, Space, Tab, and Indent Symbols

WordPerfect can display symbols for paragraphs, spaces, tabs, and indents. It's helpful to see these symbols when you're editing a document. Although you can see them on the screen, they will not print.

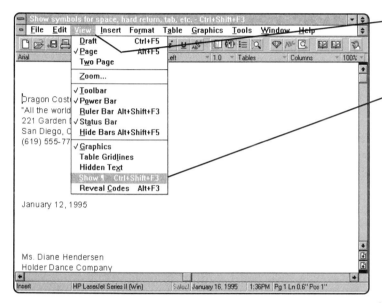

1. **Click** on **View** in the menu bar. A pull-down menu will appear.

2. **Click** on **Show ¶**. The menu will close, and the symbols will appear in your document.

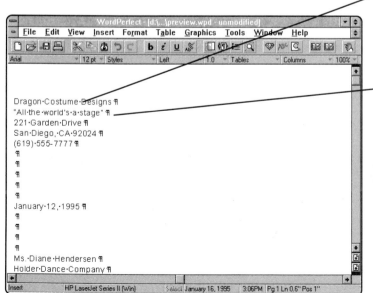

Notice the dots (·) between the words. Each dot represents a space you created by pressing the Spacebar.

Also notice the ¶ at the end of each sentence. The ¶ appears each time you press the Enter key.

Tabs are represented by an arrow. (You'll learn more about tabs in Chapter 10.)

Indents are represented by the itsy-bitsy spider (>·<).

Adding Text

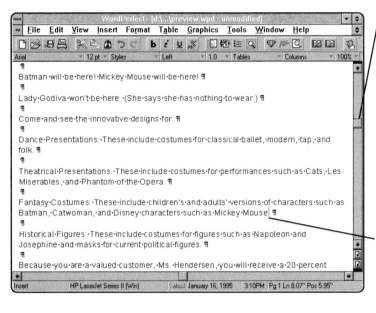

1. **Place** the **mouse arrow** on top of the scroll button. On your screen it will be at the top of the scroll bar.

2. **Press and hold** the **mouse button** to **drag** the **scroll button one third** of the way down the scroll bar. This will move you one third of the way through your document.

3. **Click** between "Mouse" and the period at the end of the "Fantasy Costumes" paragraph to place the cursor.

4. **Press** the **Spacebar** then **type** the phrase **and Donald Duck**.

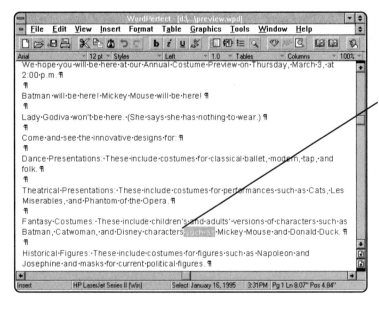

DELETING TEXT USING THE CUT BUTTON

1. **Place** the mouse pointer to the **right** of **Disney Characters** in the "Fantasy Costumes" paragraph.

2. **Press and hold** the **mouse button** and **drag** the cursor over **such as**. Be careful not to highlight the space after "as" or you will delete the space between the words.

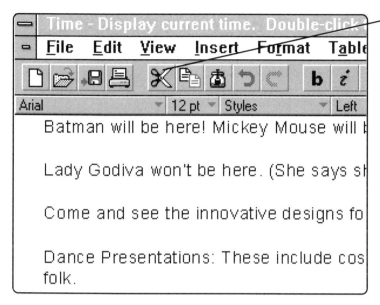

3. **Click** on the **Cut button** in the toolbar. The highlighted text will be deleted. Notice that the rest of the sentence is automatically repositioned.

UNDOING AN EDIT

If you have been following along with this chapter, you just deleted the phrase "such as." What if that was a mistake and you didn't really mean to delete those words? WordPerfect has a wonderfully forgiving feature called Edit Undo. This feature will undo your very last action as long as you don't perform any other function before you use the Undo feature.

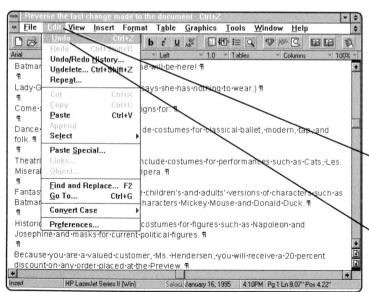

1. **Click** on **Edit** in the menu bar. A pull-down menu will appear.

2. **Click** on **Undo**. The deleted text will be restored.

Undoing an Undo

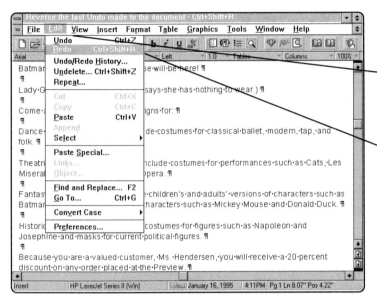

You can even undo an undo.

1. **Click** on **Edit** in the menu bar. A pull-down menu will appear.

2. **Click** on **Redo**. The deleted text will be deleted once again.

COMBINING PARAGRAPHS

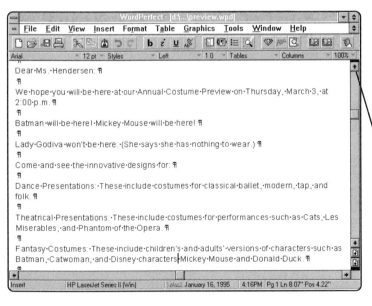

In this section you will put the Lady Godiva sentences into the preceding paragraph with Batman and Mickey Mouse.

1. **Click** on ↑ on the scroll bar to scroll up so that you can see "Dear Ms. Hendersen:"

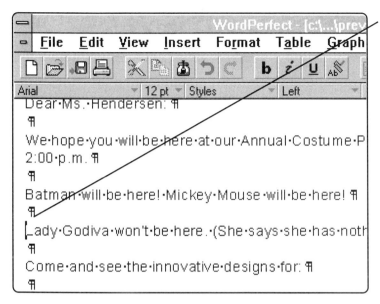

2. **Place** the **mouse pointer** at the **beginning** of the **"Lady Godiva"** sentence. **Click** to place the cursor.

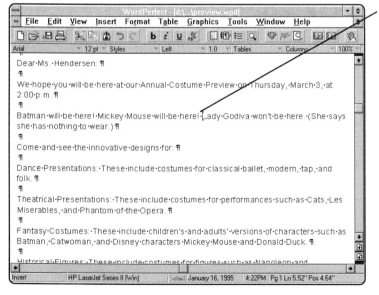

3. **Press** the **Backspace key twice**. Then **press** the **Spacebar**. This will bring the entire Lady Godiva paragraph up to the end of the Mickey Mouse sentence and put a space between the sentences.

OUTWITTING TEXT WRAP

Text wrap is the function within WordPerfect that automatically wraps long sentences to the next line. It does not always make the wrap in a place that makes sense.

It would, for example, make more sense if Les and Miserables were together on one line instead of two different lines. If you move Les to the second line with the Enter key, you will insert what is called a *hard return*. This means that this text will permanently stay as a separate line. It will not wrap back and forth between lines as you add and delete text. You can, however, move Les to the next line by inserting what WordPerfect calls a *hard space*. A hard space is seen by the computer as an actual character rather than simply a space.

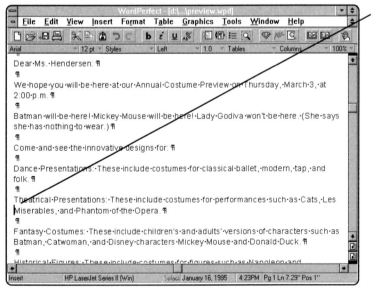

1. **Click** to the **left** of **Miserables** in the second sentence to place the cursor.

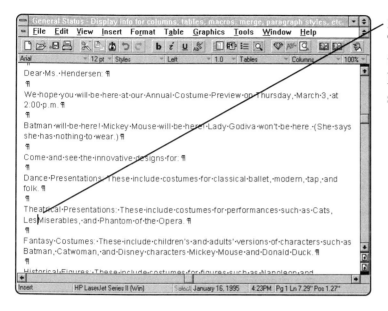

2. Press the **Backspace key**. This will bring Les down to the second line with Miserables. There will be no space between the words.

3. Click on **Format**. A pull-down menu will appear.

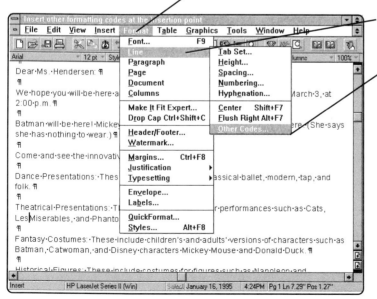

4. Click on **Line**. Another menu will appear.

5. Click on **Other Codes**. The Other Codes dialog box will appear.

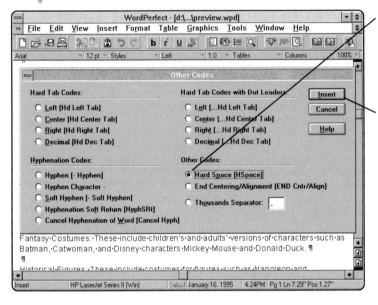

6. Click on **Hard Space [HSpace]** under the Other Codes category to insert a dot into the circle.

7. Click on **Insert**.

WordPerfect now considers Les Miserables as one word. Because Les Miserables is too long to fit on the first line, it will wrap to the second line. It will not be separated by any future text wrapping.

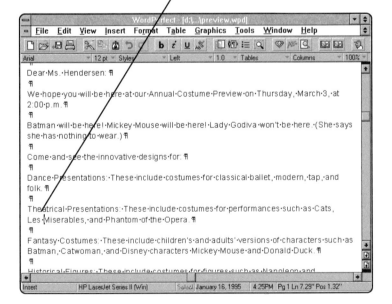

Inserting a Hard Return

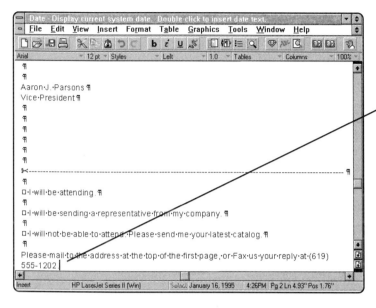

In this example, you will use a hard return to change the spacing in the very last line of the letter.

1. **Press and hold** the **Ctrl key** and **press** the **End key** (Ctrl + End). This will take you to the end of the document.

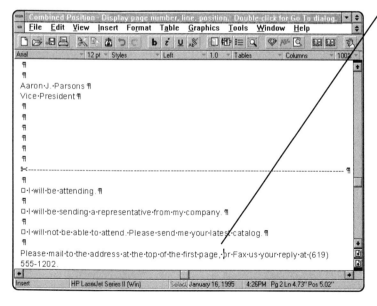

2. **Click** to the **left** of "**or**" in the last line of the letter.

3. **Press Enter**. This will move the cursor and the following text to the next line. These will now be two separate lines and will not wrap back and forth if you add or delete text.

USING THE FIND
AND REPLACE COMMAND

In this example you will replace "sen" at the end of "Hendersen" with "son." You can replace each "sen" individually, or you can use the Replace command to find and replace each occurrence for you. You will start at the top of the file since the Find and Replace command begins at the cursor and goes to the end of the file

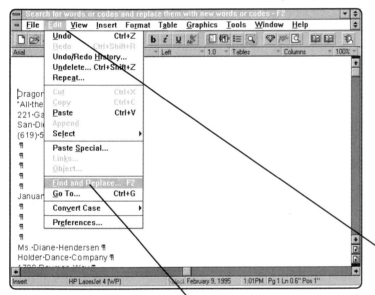

1. **Press and hold** the **Ctrl key** and **press** the **Home key** (Ctrl + Home) to go to the beginning of your file.

2. **Click** on **Edit** in the menu bar. A pull-down menu will appear.

3. **Click** on **Find and Replace**. The Find and Replace Text dialog box will appear. The cursor will be in the Find text box.

4. **Type Hendersen**.

5. **Click** in the **Replace With box** and **type Henderson**.

6. **Click** on **Replace All**. WordPerfect will replace all occurrences of Hendersen with Henderson. You will be at the end of the file.

7. **Click** on **Close**.

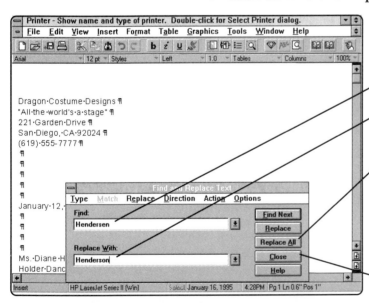

DRAG-AND-DROP MOVING

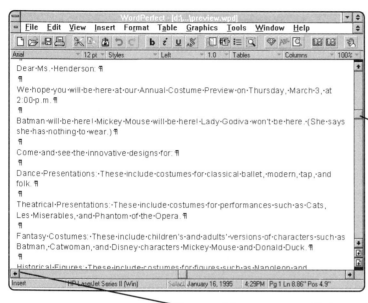

WordPerfect has a wonderful feature that lets you move text with your mouse. In this example you will move the first sentence.

1. **Click and hold** on the **scroll button** and **drag** it so that it is approximately **one-quarter** of the way from the top of the scroll bar. You should be able to see the first few paragraphs of the letter.

2. If necessary, **click** on the ◄ on the bottom scroll bar to move the screen to the right.

3. **Place** the **mouse arrow** in the **left margin** beside the first sentence.

4. **Click once** to highlight the entire sentence.

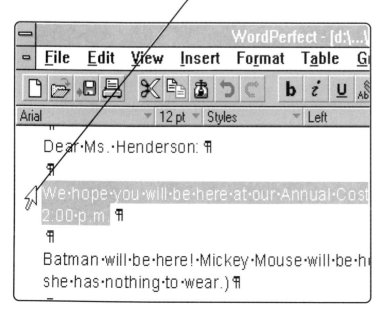

5. **Place** the **mouse arrow anywhere** on the highlighted text.

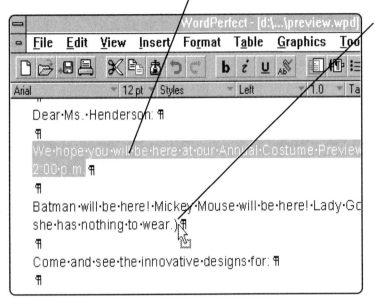

6. **Press and hold** the **mouse button** and **drag** the pointer down to the end of the next paragraph. You will see a square being dragged by the arrow. A flashing bar will appear to the right of the parenthesis.

7. **Release** the **mouse button**. The highlighted paragraph will move to that spot.

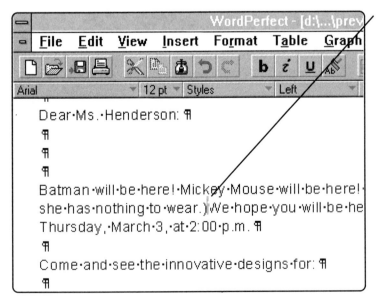

8. **Click** to the **left** of "**We**" to remove the highlighting and place the cursor.

9. **Press Enter twice** to move the "We hope" sentence to a new paragraph.

Notice there are now extra lines at the beginning of the letter.

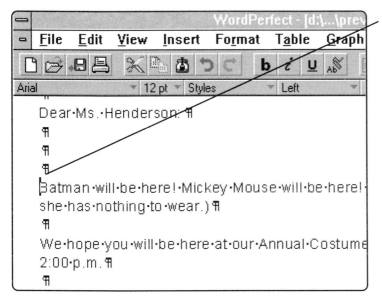

10. **Click** at the **beginning of the "Batman" sentence** to set the cursor in place.

11. **Press Backspace twice**. The text of the letter will be moved up two lines.

INSERTING A PAGE BREAK

WordPerfect does not necessarily insert an automatic page break in a place that makes sense within the context of the document. Fortunately, it's easy to change the position of the page break.

1. **Press and hold** on the **scroll button** and **drag** it halfway down the scroll bar so it looks like the one in this example. You will be able to see the automatic page break.

2. **Click** to the **left** of the "**Please return**" sentence to place the cursor.

3. **Press and hold** the **Ctrl key** as you **press Enter**. A page break will be inserted into the text at the cursor.

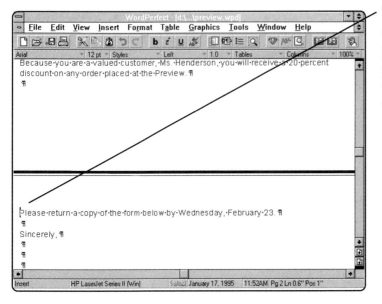

The page break will appear at the position where you placed your cursor. The previous page break that was created automatically will disappear.

DELETING A PAGE BREAK

It's very easy to delete a page break that you have inserted into the document.

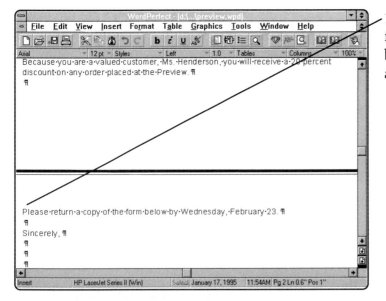

1. **Click** to the **left** of the **first line** below the page break if your cursor is not already there.

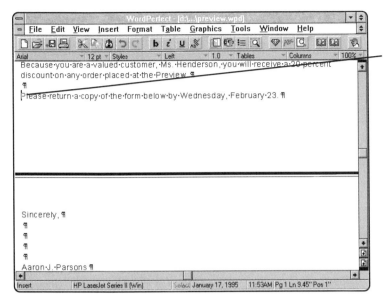

2. Press the **Backspace key**.

The text will be moved up one line and the inserted page break will disappear.

The automatic page break will reappear.

3. Press and hold the **Ctrl key** and **press Enter** to insert the page break at the "Please return" sentence again.

COPYING AND PASTING TEXT

In this three-part example you will use the Copy button, the Go To function, and the Paste button.

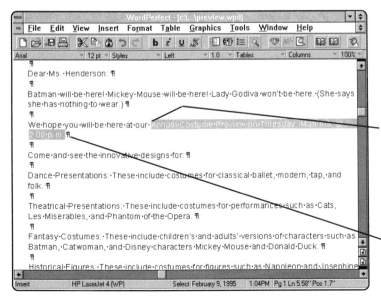

Copying the Text

1. Click repeatedly on the ⬆ on the scroll bar to bring the first sentence into view.

2. Place the **mouse pointer** immediately to the **left** of **"Annual Costume"**. The pointer should be in the shape of an I-beam.

3. Press and hold the **mouse button** as you **drag** the pointer to the end of the sentence. Both lines of text will be highlighted.

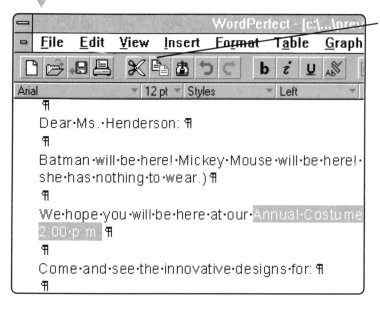

4. Click on the **Copy button** on the toolbar. You won't see any change on your screen but the highlighted text has been copied to the clipboard, a temporary storage area in your computer's memory.

Using the Go To Command

Using the Go To command is a quick way to move around in multipage documents. In this example you will use it to go to the top of page 2.

1. Click on **Edit** in the menu bar. A pull-down menu will appear.

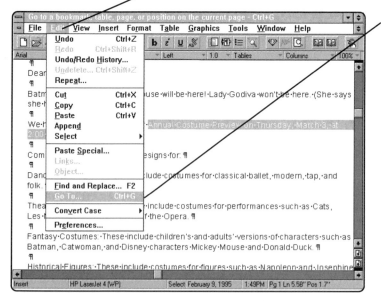

2. Click on **Go To**. The Go To dialog box will appear.

3. **Type** the number **2**. It will replace the highlighted number in the Page Number box.

4. **Click** on **OK**.

Your screen will show the top of page 2.

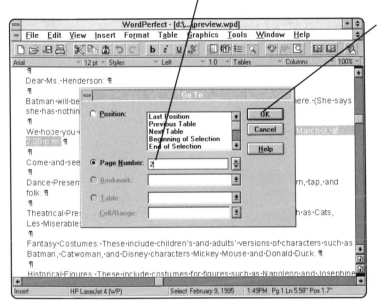

Pasting the Text

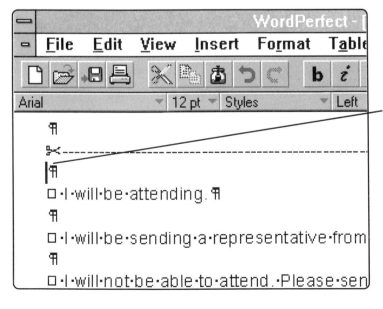

1. **Click repeatedly** on the ⬇ on the scroll bar to see the end of page 2.

2. **Click** on the **blank line** above "I will be attending."

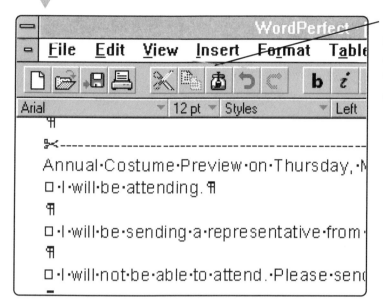

3. **Click** on the **Paste button** on the toolbar. The text you copied will be pasted into the document at the cursor, as you see in this example.

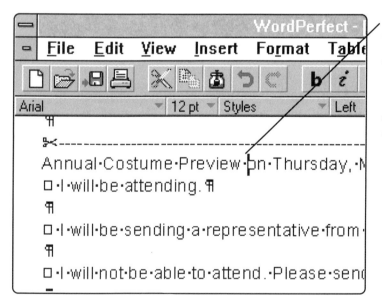

4. **Click** to the **left** of **"on Thursday"** to place the cursor.

5. **Press Enter** to move the cursor and the following text to the next line.

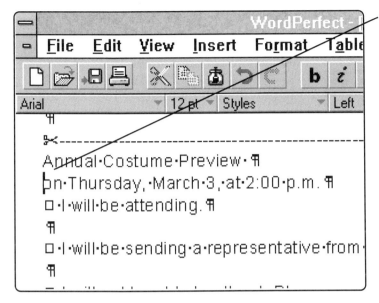

6. **Press** the **Delete key** on your keyboard three times to delete the word "on" and the space after it.

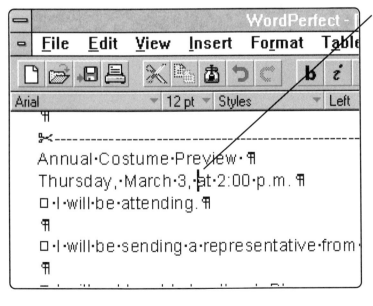

7. **Click** to the **left** of "at 2:00 p.m." to place the cursor.

8. **Press Enter** to move the text to the next line.

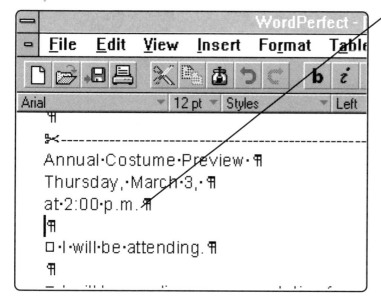

9. **Click** at the end of **p.m.** to place the cursor.

10. **Press Enter** to insert a blank line after 2:00 p.m. as you see in this example.

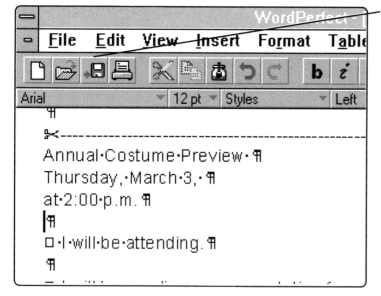

11. **Click** on the **Save button** on the toolbar to save your work.

You will use this edited letter in Part II, Formatting a Document.

Turning Off the Format Symbols

If you find the format symbols distracting, repeat steps 1-2 on page 43 to turn off the format symbols.

PART II: FORMATTING A DOCUMENT

CHAPTER

CHAPTER

7

Customizing Text

You will love how easy it is to customize the look of your text in WordPerfect 6.1. With just a few clicks of your mouse you can center text, change the type size, or make type bold, italics, or underlined. You can also create a bulleted list. In addition, you can add special borders around sections of your text then add shading inside the border to create an exciting visual effect. In this chapter, you will do the following:

✓ Change type size
✓ Convert text to upper case
✓ Make text bold, italics, and underlined
✓ Center text
✓ Create a bulleted list

CHANGING TYPE SIZE

In this section you will increase the size of the type in the first line of the letter you created in Part I. If you don't already have preview.wpd open, open it now.

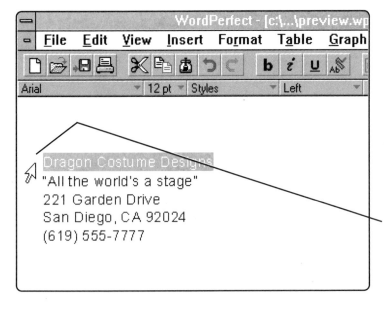

1. **Press and hold** the **Ctrl key** then **press the Home key** (Ctrl+Home) to go to the top of the file if you are not already there.

2. **Click** on the ← on the bottom scroll bar to move the screen to the right, if necessary.

3. **Click** in the left margin **beside "Dragon Costume Designs."** The line of text will be highlighted.

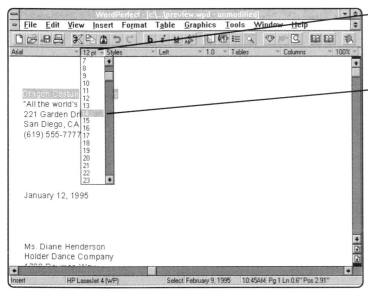

4. **Click** on the **font size button** in the toolbar. A pull-down list will appear.

5. **Click** on **14.** "Dragon Costume Designs" will change from a 12-point size to a 14-point size.

CONVERTING TEXT TO UPPER CASE

In this section you will make the text, "Dragon Costume Designs" all upper case (capital) letters.

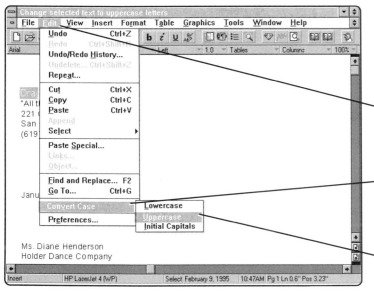

1. **Click** in the left margin beside "**Dragon Costume Designs**" if it isn't already highlighted.

2. **Click** on **Edit** in the menu bar. A pull-down menu will appear.

3. **Click** on **Convert Case**. A second menu will appear.

4. **Click** on **Uppercase**. The menu will close and the text will be all upper case.

MAKING TEXT BOLD

In this section you will make the type, "DRAGON COSTUME DESIGNS," bold.

1. **Click** in the left margin **beside "DRAGON COS- TUME DESIGNS"** to highlight it if it is not already highlighted.

2. **Click** on the **Bold button** in the toolbar. The text will be made bold. The Bold button works like a toggle switch. Click it once, and the highlighted text is made bold. Click it again while the text is highlighted and the boldface is removed. Make sure to leave the text bold.

MAKING TEXT ITALICS

In this section you will italicize the line, "All the world's a stage."

1. **Click** in the left margin **beside "All the world's a stage"** to highlight it.

2. **Click** on the **Italics button** in the toolbar. The text will be italicized. Like the Bold button, the Italics button works like a toggle switch.

UNDERLINING TEXT

In this section you will underline text.

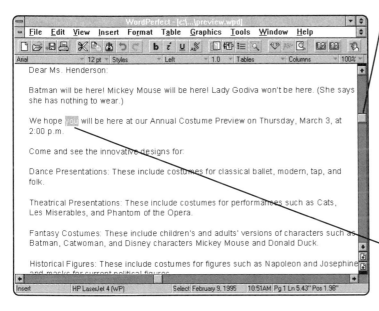

1. **Click and drag** the scroll button **one-quarter** of the way **down** the **scroll bar**. Your screen will look like the one in this example. (If you scrolled too far up or down, click on the ⬆ or ⬇ on the scroll bar until you can see approximately the same text as in the example to the left.)

2. **Place** the cursor on top of "**you**."

3. **Click twice** to highlight "**you**."

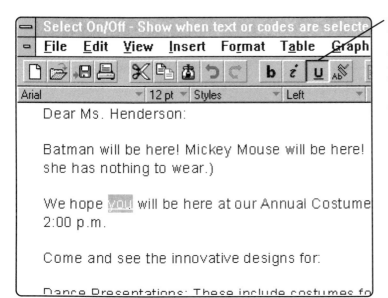

4. **Click** on the **Underline button** in the toolbar. The word "you" will be underlined.

The Underline button is another toggle switch. As you repeatedly click on it, it will turn the underlining of the highlighted text on and off.

CHECKING TEXT STYLE

In this section you will learn a method to check on the font, point size, and formatting of text.

1. **Press and hold** the **Ctrl key** then **press** the **Home key** (Ctrl+Home) to go to the top of the file.

2. **Click** to the **left** of **DRAGON** so the cursor is flashing at the beginning of the first line of text as shown.

Notice that the font and point size of 14 are indicated in the Power Bar. Notice also that the Bold button in the toolbar is pressed in.

3. **Click** to the **left** of *"All the world's a stage"* so that the cursor is flashing at the beginning of the line of text as shown.

Notice that the font and point size of 12 are indicated in the Power Bar, and the Italics button in the toolbar appears pressed in.

CENTERING TEXT
USING THE POWER BAR

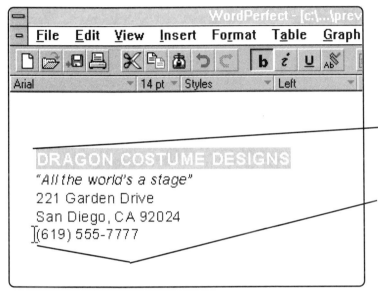

In this section you will center the company name and address. You will first highlight the lines you want to center.

1. **Click** in the left margin **next** to "**DRAGON.**" The line will be highlighted.

2. **Press and hold** the **Shift key** on your keyboard. **Click** to the **left** of "**(619) 555-7777**" with your cursor in the shape of an I-beam. All the lines between clicks will be highlighted.

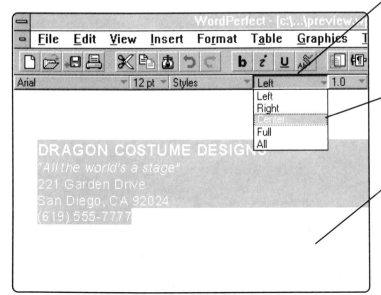

3. **Click** on the **Justification button** on the Power Bar. A pull-down menu will appear.

4. **Click** on **Center**. The menu will close, and the highlighted text will be centered.

5. **Click anywhere** on the letter to remove the high-lighting.

CENTERING TEXT USING A QUICKMENU

QuickMenus give you fast access to common commands. They are "context sensitive," which means that the list of commands depends on whether you have highlighted text or have simply placed the cursor next to the text.

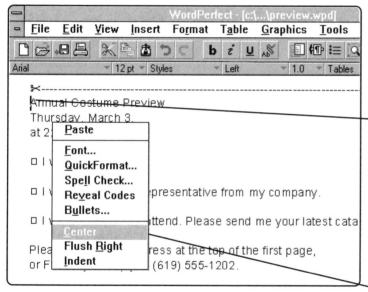

1. **Click and hold** on the **scroll button** and **drag** it **three-quarters** of the way **down** the **scroll bar** so that you can see the scissors.

2. **Click** to the **left** of "**Annual Costume Preview**" with your cursor in the shape of an I-beam.

3. **Click** the *right* **mouse button**. A QuickMenu will appear.

4. **Click** on **Center**. The menu will close, and the text will be centered.

5. **Repeat steps 2 - 4** to center "**Thursday, March 3**," and "**at 2:00 p.m.**" Your screen will look like this example.

CENTERING TEXT
USING THE LAYOUT MENU

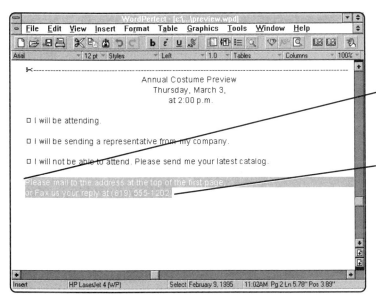

In this section you'll use a third method, the layout menu, to center text.

1. **Click** to the **left** of "**Please mail**" at the bottom of the letter.

2. **Press and hold** the **mouse button** and **drag** the highlight to the end of "**(619) 555-1202.**"

3. **Click** on **Format** in the menu bar. A pull-down menu will appear.

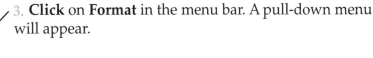

4. **Click** on **Justification**. A second menu will appear.

5. **Click** on **Center**. The menus will disappear, and your document screen will appear with the highlighted text centered.

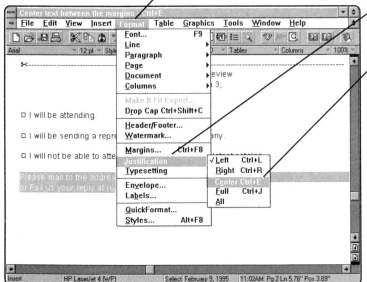

UNDOING TEXT ALIGNMENT

In this example you will change text that is center-aligned to make it left-aligned. Then you will undo the change.

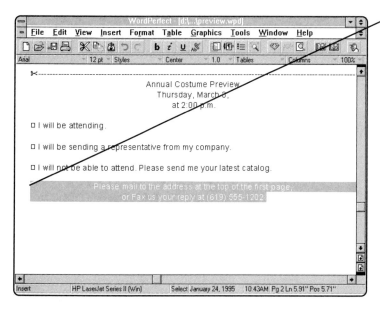

1. **Repeat steps 1 and 2** of the **previous section** if the last two lines of the letter are not already highlighted.

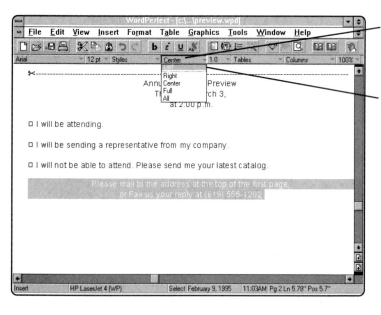

2. **Click** on the **Justification button** on the Power Bar. A pull-down menu will appear.

3. **Click** on **Left**. The two lines of text will be left-aligned.

Since you want the text centered instead of left-aligned, you need to undo your last move.

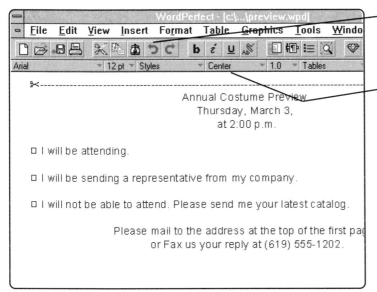

4. **Click** on the **Undo button** in the toolbar. The text will be center-aligned again.

Notice that the Justification button now shows "Center" instead of "Left" to indicate the highlighted text is center-aligned.

Now would be a good time to save your changes. You should get into the habit of saving while you work.

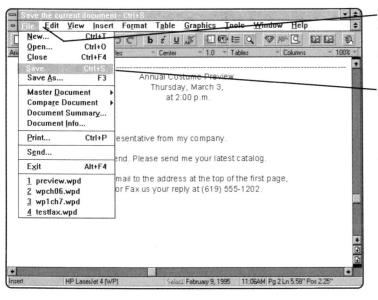

5. **Click** on **File** in the menu bar. A pull-down menu will appear.

6. **Click** on **Save**. The changes will be saved, and you will be returned to the document screen. (Remember you can also click on the Save button in the toolbar.)

CREATING A BULLETED LIST

In this section, with a few clicks of your mouse, you will create a bulleted list using the four paragraphs describing the costumes carried by Dragon Costume Designs.

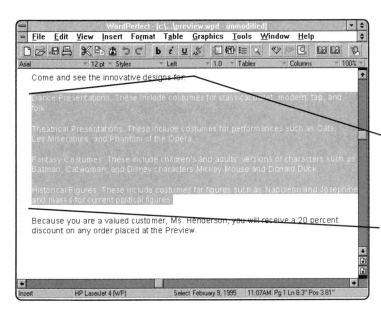

1. Drag the **scroll button up** the scroll bar so you can see the paragraphs that describe the innovative costume designs.

2. Click in the left margin **beside "Dance Presentations."** The paragraph will be highlighted.

3. Press and hold the **mouse button**, and **drag** the cursor down to the "**Historical**" paragraph. The four paragraphs will be highlighted.

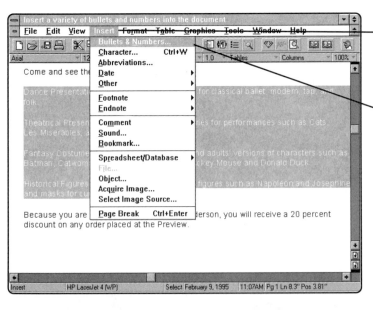

4. Click on the **Insert** in the menu bar. A pull-down menu will appear.

5. Click on **Bullets & Numbers**. The Bullets & Numbers dialog box will appear.

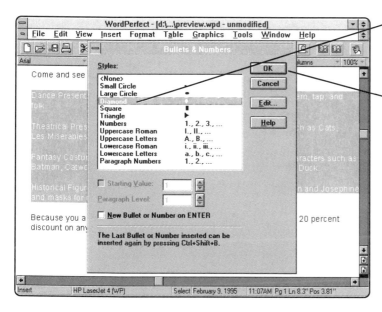

6. **Click** on **Diamond** to select a diamond-shaped bullet for your bulleted list.

7. **Click** on **OK**. The Bullets & Numbers dialog box will disappear, and the four paragraphs you highlighted will be in the form of a bulleted list. Pretty neat!

8. **Click anywhere** on the document to remove the highlighting.

DELETING A BULLET

1. **Click** to the **left** of "**Historical Figures**."

2. **Press** the **Backspace key**. The bullet will be deleted, and the paragraph will be aligned at the left margin.

Use the Undo feature to restore the bullet.

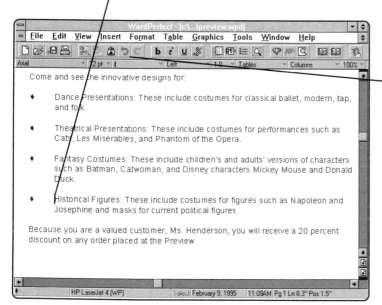

3. **Click** on the **Undo button** in the toolbar. The bullet will be restored.

SAVING YOUR WORK

You definitely need to save after all this work.

1. **Click** on the **Save button** in the toolbar.

Adding Pictures and Creating TextArt

Whether you call them pictures, images, clip art, or graphics, a visual element can add impact and interest to your document. Although WordPerfect comes with some interesting images, you can purchase some really cool collections separately through WordPerfect. Call their customer service line. In this chapter, you will do the following:

✔ Insert an image into a document
✔ Change the text wrap
✔ Reposition and resize an image
✔ Create TextArt
✔ Reposition and resize TextArt

PREPARING TO PLACE A PICTURE

In this example, you'll use one of three methods to add a picture to your document. Using the Drag to Create method gives you more control over size and position when you first place the picture.

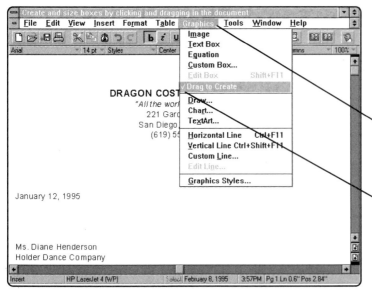

1. **Press and hold** the **Ctrl key** and **press** the **Home key** (Ctrl + Home) to place your cursor at the beginning of the file, if necessary.

2. **Click** on **Graphics** in the menu bar. A pull-down menu will appear.

3. **Click** on **Drag to Create** to *place* a ✔ in the list, *only* if one isn't there already. If a ✔ is there and you click on it, you'll remove it.

PLACING A PICTURE

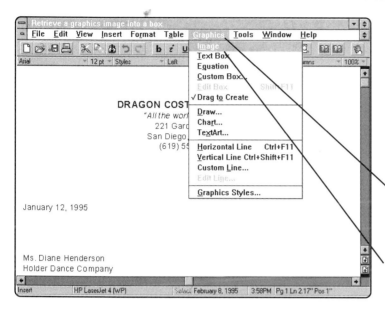

Creating an Image Box

Using the Image command lets you create an Image Box (placement area) for pictures in your document.

1. **Click** on **Graphics**. A pull-down menu will appear.

2. **Click** on **Image**. The menu will close.

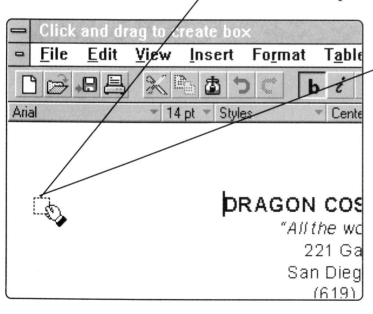

3. **Move** the **mouse pointer** onto the document. The pointer will look like a hand holding a dotted box.

4. **Place** the **pointer** in line with "Dragon Costume Designs" as you see in this example. You don't need to be exact at this point. You'll reposition the graphic later in this chapter.

5. **Press and hold** the **mouse button** as you **drag** the cursor down and to the right. A dotted outline will appear as you drag, defining the size of the Image Box in which the picture will appear.

6. **Release** the **mouse button** when the outline is like the one you see in this example. The Insert Image dialog box will appear.

Choosing a Picture

Notice the list of 81 WordPerfect Graphic (.wpg) files which are contained in WordPerfect's graphics folder.

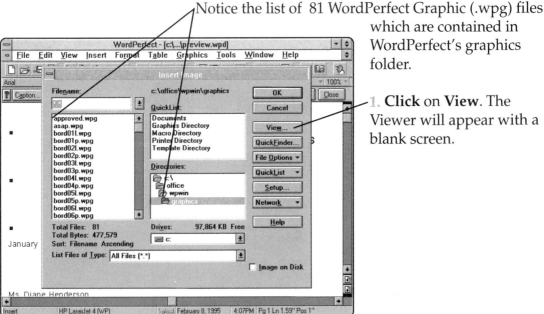

1. **Click** on **View**. The Viewer will appear with a blank screen.

2. **Click repeatedly** on the ⬇ to the right of the filename list to scroll through the list.

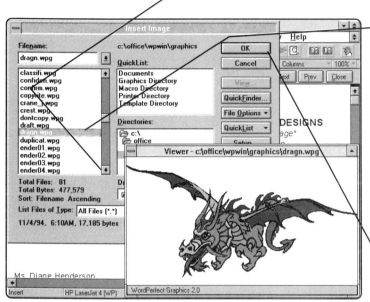

3. **Click** on **dragn.wpg**. The image will appear in the Viewer as you see in this example.

4. **Scroll through** the list, and click on any other pictures you'd like to view. Just remember to click on dragn.wpg again before continuing.

5. **Click** on **OK**. The Insert Image dialog box will close. The image will appear in the Image Box in the document.

CHANGING TEXT WRAP

You've undoubtedly seen ads in magazines where the text curls around the picture. You can do this in WordPerfect 6.1 with the Wrap Text feature. In this section, you'll use the No Wrap command.

Notice the solid squares, or handles, surrounding the picture. The handles indicate the size of the Image Box, and show that the image is selected (ready for editing).

Notice that the top five lines of text have shifted position. The Image Box, in which the dragn.wpg was placed, has a square text wrap automatically assigned to it.

Notice that the Graphics Box feature bar has appeared under the Power Bar.

1. **Click** on **Wrap**. The Wrap Text dialog box will appear.

2. **Click** on **No Wrap (through)** to place a dot in the circle. This will cause the text to print *on top* of the Image Box (rectangle) surrounding the graphic.

3. **Click** on **OK**. The dialog box will close.

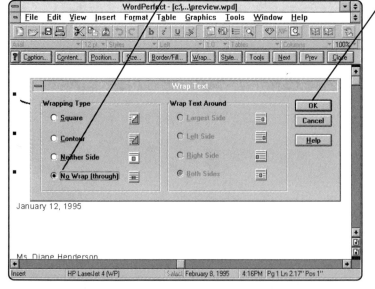

Notice that the text has returned to its original, centered position. If you had not centered the five lines of the address back in Chapter 7, they would have appeared directly on top of the dragon. In other words, they would have printed *through* the dragon. However, this text is centered, so it prints through the edge of the box only.

4. **Click anywhere** on the document to remove the dragon's handles. Your screen will look like this example.

MOVING A GRAPHIC

No matter how careful you are, the size and position of graphics always seem to need some fine tuning. In this section, you'll select the dragon once again before moving him (or her).

1. **Move** the **cursor** around on the graphic. At some point, the I-beam will become a white arrow. The exact point can be tricky to find at first.

2. Press and hold the **mouse button**. The white arrow will become a four-headed arrow, and the handles will appear around the picture.

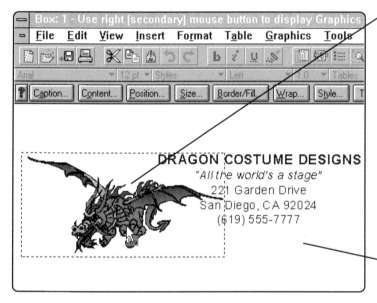

3. Continue to **hold** the **mouse button** as you **drag** the picture down slightly, so that the top of the dotted box around the dragon aligns with the top of the text in "DRAGON COSTUME DESIGNS" as you see here.

4. Release the **mouse button** when the dotted box is in position.

5. Click anywhere to remove the handles.

RESIZING A GRAPHIC

You can increase or decrease the size of the graphic.

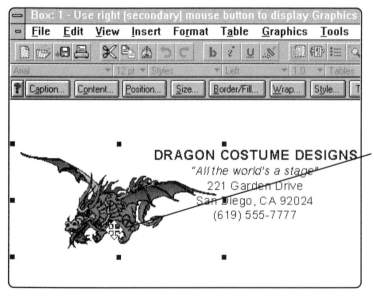

1. Move the **cursor** around on the graphic. At some point, the I-beam will become a white arrow. The exact point may be difficult to find, but it is there.

2. When the cursor is a white arrow, **click** the **mouse button**. The white arrow will become a four-headed arrow, and the handles will appear around the picture.

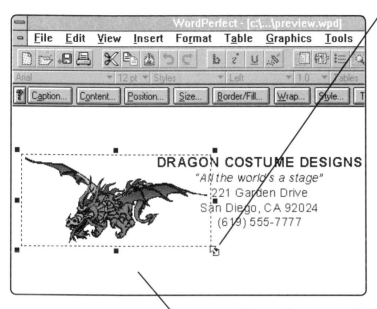

3. **Place** the **cursor** on the bottom right square of the Image Box. The cursor will undergo yet another transformation into a two-headed arrow. You may have to fiddle with the placement to get the cursor to change into the right shape.

4. **Press and hold** as you **drag** the **cursor** slightly up and to the left to resize the dragon to about the size you see here.

5. **Release** the **mouse button**.

6. **Click anywhere** to remove the dragon's handles.

DELETING A GRAPHIC

1. **Repeat steps 1 - 2** in the previous section to select the graphic.

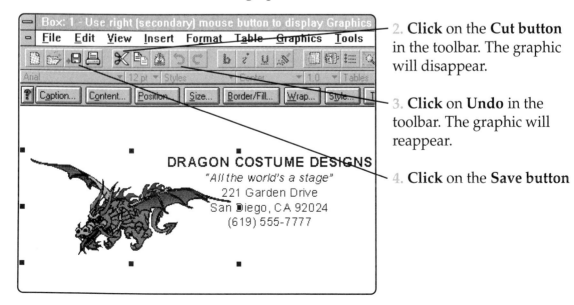

2. **Click** on the **Cut button** in the toolbar. The graphic will disappear.

3. **Click** on **Undo** in the toolbar. The graphic will reappear.

4. **Click** on the **Save button**

CREATING TEXTART

Sometimes a document needs just a little extra pizzazz. Using a special subprogram, WordPerfect lets you create art with words. In this section, you'll replace "Annual Costume Preview" with TextArt.

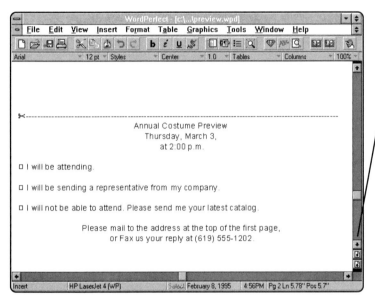

1. **Press and hold** the **Ctrl key,** and **press** the **End key** (Ctrl + End) to place your cursor at the end of the file, if necessary.

2. **Click** twice on the ↓ on the scroll bar so that your screen resembles this example.

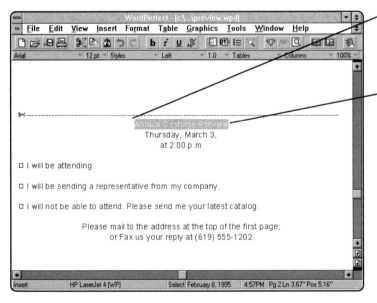

3. **Click** to the **left** of "**Annual Costume Preview**" to place the cursor.

4. **Press and hold** the **mouse button** and **drag** the cursor to the right to highlight the words.

5. **Press** the **Delete key** on your keyboard. "Annual Costume Preview" will disappear.

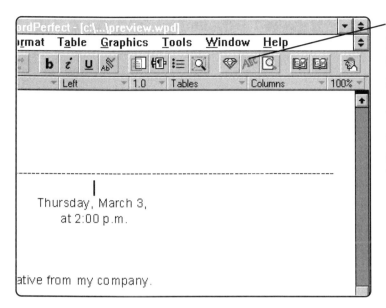

6. **Click** on the **TextArt button** (ABC) on the toolbar. It's the fifth button from the right.

Your screen will go through some contortions. Eventually, the TextArt window will appear.

Notice that "Text" is already highlighted and can be seen surrounded by an outline with black squares, or handles.

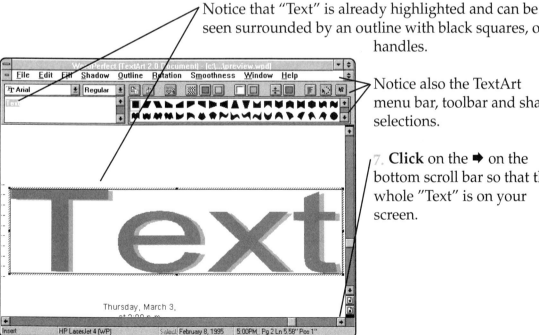

Notice also the TextArt menu bar, toolbar and shape selections.

7. **Click** on the ➡ on the bottom scroll bar so that the whole "Text" is on your screen.

ENTERING AND STYLING
TEXT IN TEXTART

If you're lucky enough to have a color printer, feel free to choose more vibrant colors than we do in this section. With standard printers, shades of gray are as lively as we can get.

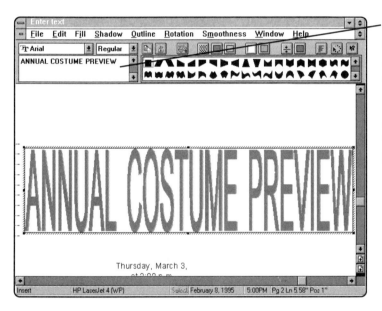

1. **Type ANNUAL COSTUME PREVIEW.** It will replace the highlighted "Text."

After a pause, the new text will appear in the text block as you see here.

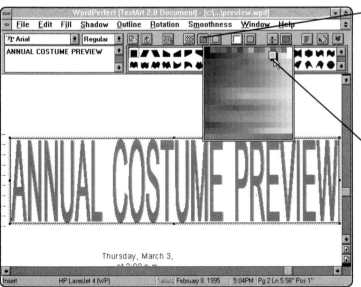

2. **Click** on the **Text pattern foreground color button** in the toolbar. It's the fifth button from the left. A pull-down color selector will appear.

3. **Click** on the **gray square**, second row, fourth from the right. The text foreground will change to gray.

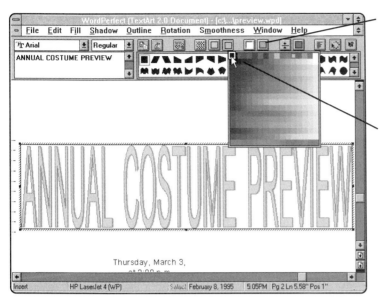

4. **Click** on the **Shadow color button** in the toolbar. It's the sixth from the right. A pull-down color selector will appear.

5. **Click** on the **black square** in the upper left corner. The shadow will change to black.

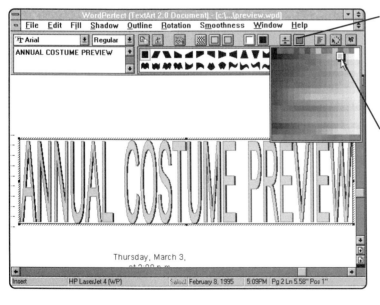

6. **Click** on the **Text outline color button** in the toolbar. It's the fourth from the right. A pull-down color selector will appear.

7. **Click** on the **gray square**, second row, fourth from the right. The line color will change to gray.

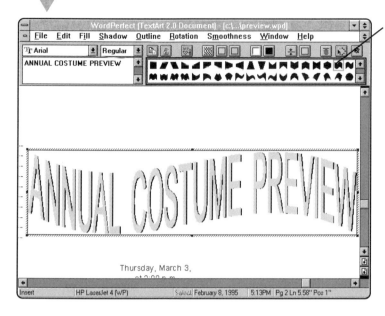

8. Click on the **shape** figure, top row, second from the right. After a brief pause, the text will be reshaped as you see in this example.

INSERTING TEXTART

Frankly, this next section is tough. When trying to mix TextArt and regular text, the TextArt takes on a life of its own. We found that it takes a great deal of patience and persistence to position TextArt precisely in a document.

Sizing TextArt

1. Move the **mouse pointer** onto the top middle handle of the border. The pointer will become a two-headed arrow.

2. Press and hold the **mouse button** as you **drag** the border down about an inch.

3. Release the **mouse button**. The TextArt will be resized.

Moving TextArt

1. **Place** the **mouse pointer** on the border of the TextArt (*not* on the black handle.) A four-headed arrow will appear beneath the pointer.

2. **Press and hold** the **mouse button** as you **drag** the border up and to the left. Place it on top of the date and time, as you see here.

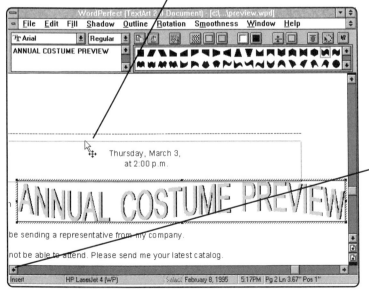

3. **Release** the **mouse button**. The TextArt will appear in a new position. It's probably not exactly where you wanted it, but it's in a new position, nonetheless.

4. **Click** on the ◆ on the bottom scroll bar to move your screen back into position if it has scrolled over.

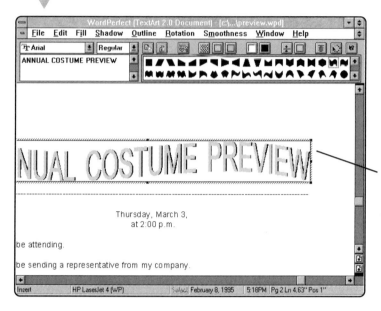

The goal is to place the "ANNUAL COSTUME PREVIEW" TextArt between the dotted line and "Thursday, March 3." And for some reason, it doesn't want to do what it's told.

5. Repeat steps **2-3** as often as necessary. Annoying, isn't it?

Sizing TextArt

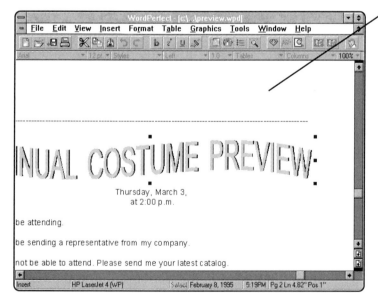

1. Click anywhere on the **document** in the background. The TextArt program will close.

You can size and move the TextArt here as needed.

Adding a Filled Border and a Customized Line

In addition to clip art images and TextArt, WordPerfect gives you other ways to dress up your document. Borders can be placed around columns, pages and/or paragraphs, and lines can be customized and inserted anywhere your heart desires. In this chapter, you will do the following:

✔ Add a filled border to a paragraph
✔ Customize and add a line

ADDING A FILLED BORDER TO A PARAGRAPH

Borders can be added to any element in your document. In this example, you'll add a border to a single paragraph.

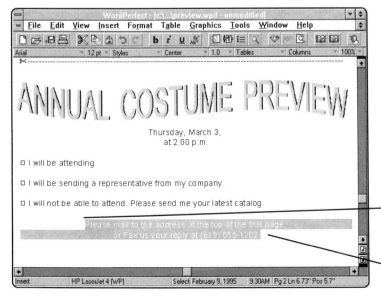

1. **Press and hold** the **Ctrl key**, and **press** the **End key** (Ctrl + End) to go to the end of the file, if you're not already there.

2. **Click** on the ↓ on the scroll bar to adjust your screen as necessary.

3. **Click** to the **left** of "**Please mail**."

4. **Press and hold** the **mouse button** and **drag** the highlight bar to the **end** of "**(619) 555-1202**."

5. **Click** on **Format** in the menu bar. A pull-down menu will appear.

6. **Click** on **Paragraph**. A second menu will appear.

7. **Click** on **Border/Fill**. The Paragraph Border dialog box will appear.

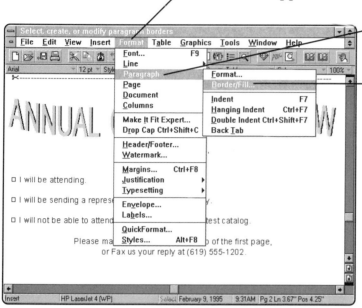

8. **Click** on the **Border Styles button** under Border Options. A selection of border styles will appear.

9. **Click** on the **double line** border style, third row from the top, first column on the left.

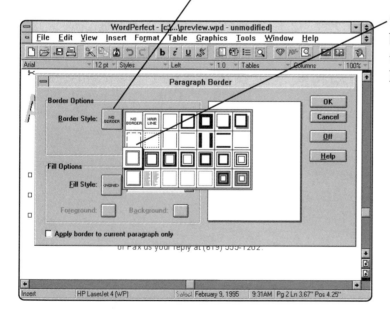

10. Click on the **Fill Style button** under Fill Options. A selection of Fill Styles will appear.

11. Click on the **5% fill** style, top row, second from the left.

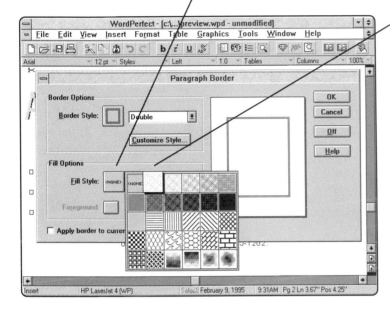

Notice that the styles you selected are shown in the preview box.

12. Click on **OK**. The Paragraph Border dialog box will close.

13. Click anywhere to remove the highlighting. Your screen will look like this example.

REMOVING A FILLED BORDER

In this example, you decide that the filled border makes the page too "busy." No problem, it's easy to remove. You can, of course, use the Undo button if you haven't done any other action, but this example will teach you how to remove a filled border at any time.

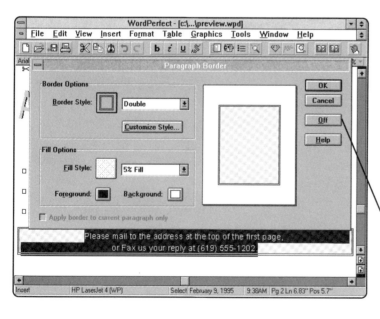

1. Repeat steps 3-7 in the previous section to highlight the two lines of type at the bottom of page 2, and open the Paragraph Border dialog box.

2. Click on **Off**. You will be returned to your document screen, and the filled border will be removed.

ADDING A CUSTOMIZED LINE

WordPerfect considers lines as separate graphics, just like clip art or TextArt. In this example, you'll customize and add a line to page 1.

1. **Press and hold** the **Ctrl key**, and **press** the **Home key** (Ctrl + Home) to go to the top of the file, if you're not already there.

2. **Click** to **place** the cursor 3 lines above "January 12, 1995."

3. **Click** on **Graphics** in the menu bar. A pull-down menu will appear.

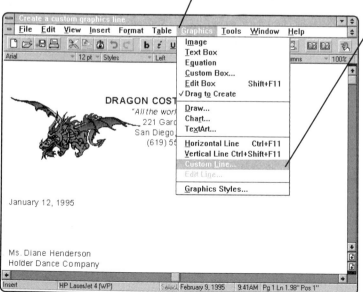

4. **Click** on **Custom Line**. The Create Graphics Line dialog box will appear.

5. **Click** on the **Line Style button**. A selection of Line Styles will appear.

6. **Click** on **Thick**, bottom row, first on the left.

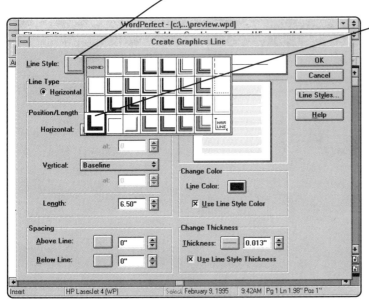

Notice that the line style and position are previewed.

7. **Click** on the **Line Color button** under Change Color. A selection of line colors will appear.

8. **Click** on the **gray square**, second row, fourth from the right.

9. **Click** on **OK**. The dialog box will close, and a line will appear in your document.

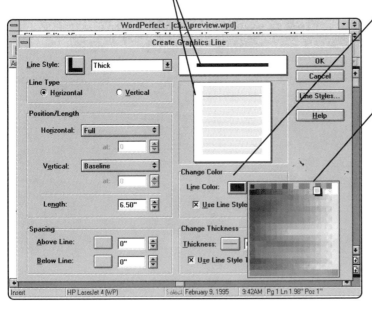

Your screen will look like this example.

REMOVING A CUSTOMIZED LINE

1. **Place** the **mouse pointer on top** of the line to be deleted.

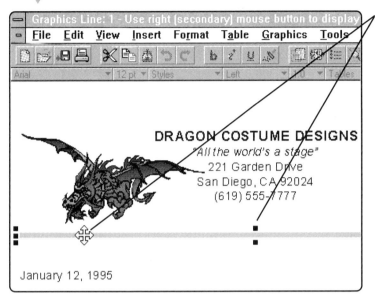

2. **Click** the **mouse button**. The pointer will become a four-headed arrow, and the line will be surrounded by black squares, or handles.

3. **Press** the **Delete key** on your keyboard. The line will disappear.

4. **Click** on the **Undo button** on the toolbar. The line will be restored.

Lines are moved and sized just like graphics. See Chapter 7, "Adding Pictures and Creating TextArt" for more information.

CHAPTER 10

Setting Tabs

WordPerfect has tabs preset every half-inch. To insert a tab, simply press the Tab key. You can also set your own tabs. When you set a tab, it is set from that point on for the rest of the document until you reset the tabs. You can reset tabs as many times as you like within a document. In this chapter you will change the line spacing to double space, and set and apply the following kinds of tabs:

✔ A *left-aligned tab* that aligns words or numbers on the first character: Josh
                                                           Jessica

✔ A *leader* (line) that ends at a right-aligned tab: Josh_____
                                            Jessica_____

✔ A *right-aligned tab* that aligns words or numbers on the last character: Josh
                                                     Jessica

✔ A *center-aligned tab* that centers words or numbers: Josh
                                          Jessica

✔ A *decimal tab* that aligns numbers on the decimal point: 13.95
                                          105.00

DISPLAYING THE RULER BAR

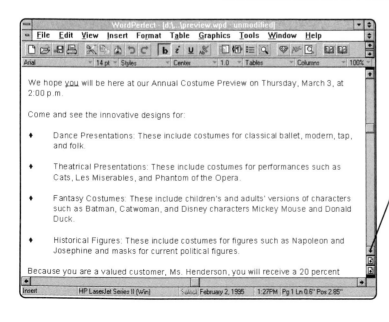

In this example you will display the ruler bar, which is a wonderfully helpful feature when you're setting tabs.

1. **Open preview.wpd** if it isn't already on your screen.

2. **Click repeatedly** on the ⬇ on the scroll bar to position your screen like the one you see here.

3. **Click** on **View** in the menu bar. A pull-down menu will appear.

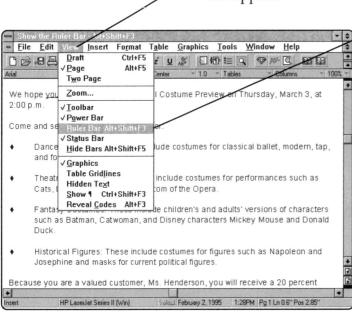

4. **Click** on **Ruler Bar**. The ruler bar will appear below the Power bar.

RESETTING TABS
FOR A BULLETED LIST

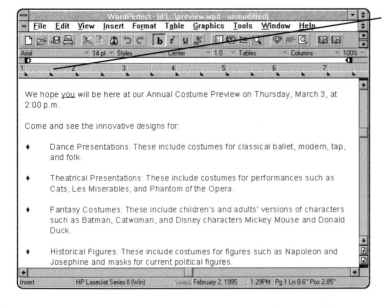

Notice the left-aligned tab marks every half-inch.

In a bulleted list, the paragraph is indented a tab width (the pre-set half inch) to the right of the bullet. You can, however, change the space between the bullet and the paragraph by simply resetting the tab. First, you will clear the existing tabs.

Clearing Existing Tabs

1. **Click** on the **blank line** above the first bulleted paragraph.

2. **Click** on **Format** in the menu bar. A pull-down menu will appear.

3. **Click** on **Line**. A second menu will appear.

4. **Click** on **Tab Set**. The Tab Set dialog box will appear.

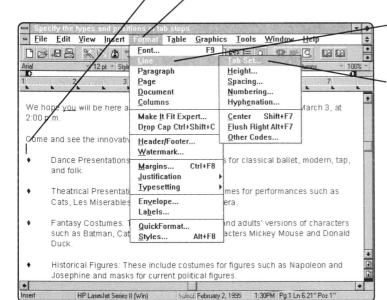

5. **Click** on **Clear All**.

6. **Click** on **OK**. This will clear all the tabs from the cursor through the rest of the document.

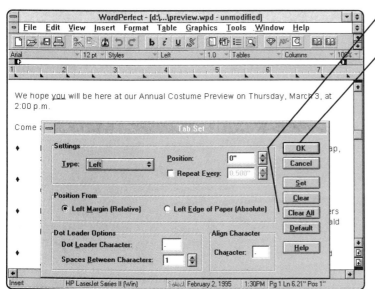

Notice that the tab marks on the ruler have disappeared.

Notice also that the paragraphs have dropped down a line. This will be remedied when you place the tab.

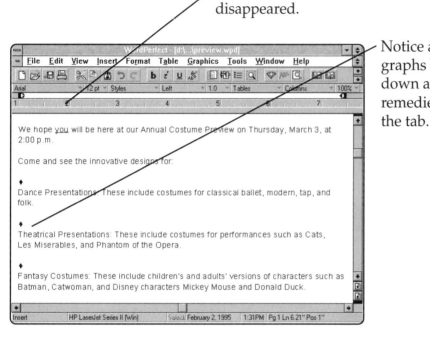

SETTING A LEFT-ALIGNED TAB WITH THE MOUSE

In this example you will set a tab ¹/₄ inch from the left margin. Because the left margin is 1 inch wide, the tab will be set at the 1¹/₄ inch mark on the ruler.

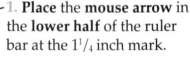

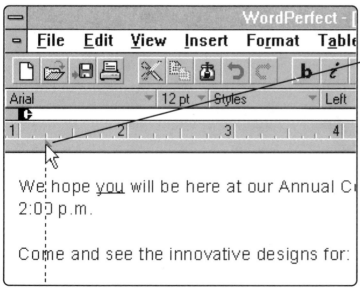

1. **Place** the **mouse arrow** in the **lower half** of the ruler bar at the 1¹/₄ inch mark.

2. **Press and hold** the **mouse button**. You will see a dotted line appear in your letter at the 1¹/₄ inch mark. The dotted line allows you to check the placement of the tab in relation to the text.

3. Release the **mouse button**. A left-aligned tab mark will appear at the 1¼ inch mark. This tab is set for the rest of the document until you change it.

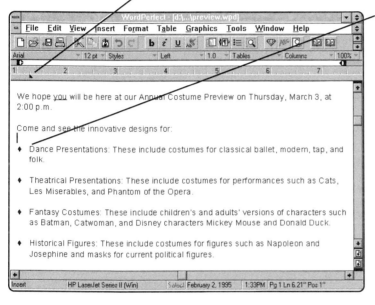

Notice that the bulleted paragraphs are now indented ¼ inch from the left margin.

USING A PRE-SET TAB

In this example, you'll use the left-aligned tab you set in the last example.

1. Press and hold the **Ctrl key** then **press** the **End key** (Ctrl + End) to go to the end of the file.

2. Click on the blank line **above "I will not be able to attend."** On your screen it will be blank.

3. Press the **Tab key** and **type Name**.

SETTING A RIGHT-ALIGNED TAB

In this section you'll use the Tab Set dialog box to insert a solid line (or leader) after "Name." Using a right-aligned tab ensures that it ends at a specific spot.

1. **Click** on **Format** in the menu bar. A pull-down menu will appear.

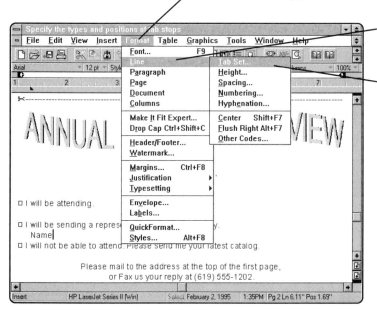

2. **Click** on **Line**. Another pull-down menu will appear.

3. **Click** on **Tab Set**. The Tab Set dialog box will appear.

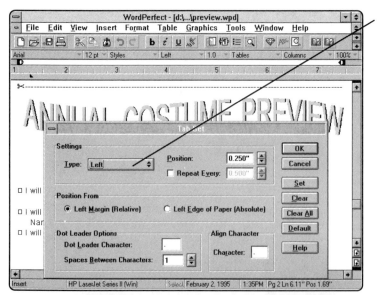

4. **Press and hold** on **Left** in the Type box. A pull-down menu will appear.

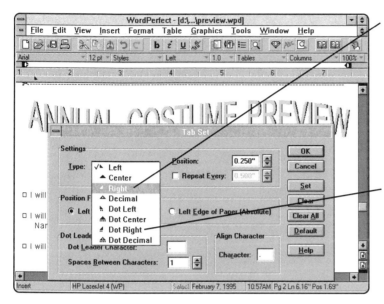

5. **Continue to hold** the **mouse button** and **drag** the highlight bar down to **Right**, then **release** the **mouse button**. The pull-down menu will disappear, and Right will appear in the Type box.

If you wanted a dotted-line leader (like you see in a Table of Contents) you would highlight Dot Right.

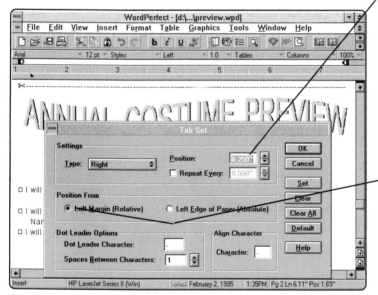

6. **Place** the **mouse pointer** in the **Position box**. It will be in the shape of an I-beam.

7. **Click twice**. The 0.250" will be highlighted.

8. **Type 4**. It will replace the highlighted number.

Notice that Left Margin (Relative) is pre-selected (already has a dot in the circle). *Relative* means the tab is set in relation to the left margin. If you change the left margin, the tab will stay the same distance from the new left margin. An *absolute* tab, on the other hand, is measured from the edge of the paper. If you change the margin, the distance from the edge of the paper to the tab does not change.

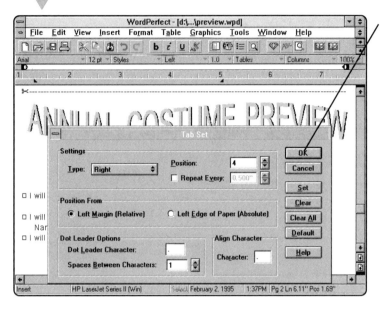

9. **Click** on **OK**. The dialog box will close.

Now you have a right-aligned tab set at 4 inches. However, you still have to set up the solid line (underline) feature.

10. **Click** on **Format** in the menu bar. A pull-down menu will appear.

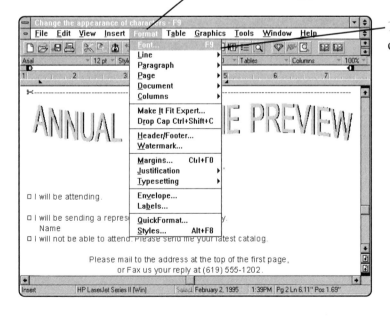

11. **Click** on **Font**. The Font dialog box will appear.

12. Click on **Tabs** to insert an ✕ in the box. This tells WordPerfect to underline the space between tabs.

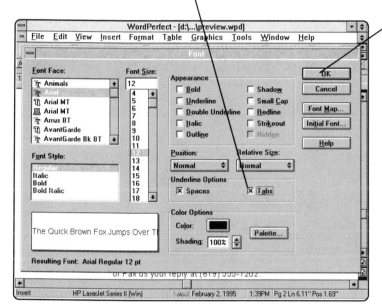

13. Click on **OK**. The dialog box will close.

There's one more step in this process.

14. Click on the **Underline button** in the toolbar to turn the underline function on. The button will appear pressed in. (As long as the Underline button is pressed in, tabs will be underlined. You will turn off the underline function in the next section.)

Notice the right-aligned tab mark on the ruler at the 5-inch mark.

Now, you're finally ready to insert the right-aligned leader line.

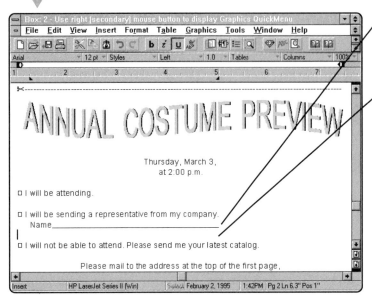

15. Press the **Tab key** on your keyboard. The leader will be inserted into the text.

16. Press Enter to move the insertion point to a new line.

SETTING AN EXACT TAB

When you set a tab with the mouse, it may or may not be at an exact position. You may get a tab at .244 inches, for example, rather than .25 inches. In most cases this difference doesn't matter. If you need to set a tab at a precise position, however, use the Tab Set dialog box.

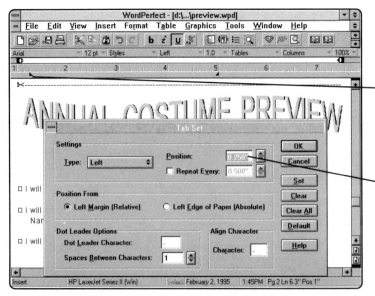

In this example, you'll set a left-aligned tab at precisely .5 inches.

1. Click twice on any **tab mark** in the ruler. This is another way to open the Tab Set dialog box.

2. Click twice in the **Position Box**. The .250" in the box will be highlighted.

3. **Type .5** to set the tab at exactly $\frac{1}{2}$ inch. It will replace the .250".

4. **Confirm** that **Left** is in the Type box.

5. **Click** on **OK**. The dialog box will close.

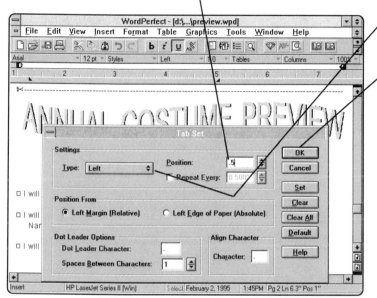

Notice that you now have two tabs set—one at $\frac{1}{4}$ inch and one at $\frac{1}{2}$ inch.

6. **Click** on the **Underline button** in the toolbar. Because the underline function is turned on when the button is pressed in, clicking on the button again will turn *off* the underline function.

7. **Press** the **Tab key** on your keyboard **twice** to tab to the $\frac{1}{2}$ inch mark.

8. **Type Title**.

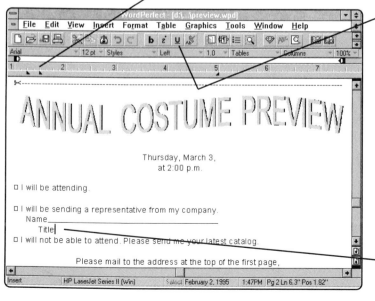

Now you have to turn the underline function on once again.

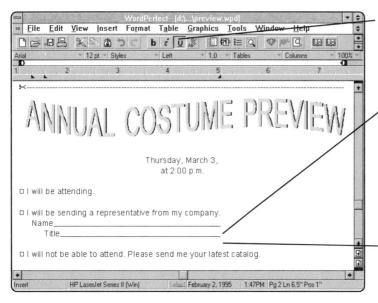

9. **Click** on the **Underline button** in the toolbar to turn it on. The button will appear pressed in on your screen.

10. **Press** the **Tab key** on your keyboard once. You will tab to the next tab position, which is a right-aligned tab at the 5-inch mark.

11. **Press Enter** to move the insertion point to the next line.

DELETING A TAB

In this example you will delete the tab you set at the .5 inch mark.

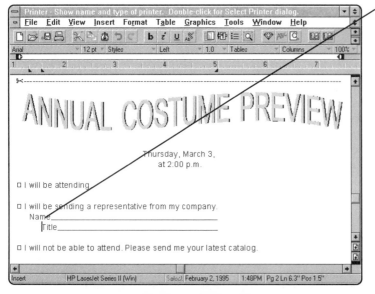

1. **Click** to the **left** of **Title** to set the cursor.

2. **Press** the **Backspace key** on your keyboard. The word "Title" will be backspaced to align under "Name." Notice that the underline automatically extends to the right-aligned tab at 5 inches.

3. **Click and hold** on the $^1/_2$ **inch tab mark** in the ruler bar.

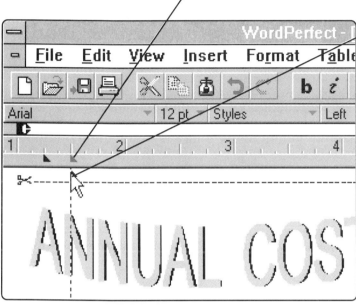

4. **Continue to hold** the **mouse button** and **drag** the tab marker down into the document page.

5. **Release** the **mouse button**. The tab will be removed from the ruler bar. (Isn't this a really cool feature?)

6. **Press and hold** the **Ctrl key** then **type** the letter **s** (Ctrl + s) to save your work. (This is another way to save.)

OPENING A NEW DOCUMENT

In the remaining sections of the chapter, you'll review setting right-aligned tabs. You will also learn how to set a center-aligned tab and a decimal tab. Since the tabs will not be used in the preview.wpd letter, you will open a new document. You don't need to close preview.wpd in order to open a new document. WordPerfect allows up to nine documents to be open at a time.

1. **Click** on the **New Document button** in the toolbar. A new document screen will appear.

SETTING A RIGHT-ALIGNED TAB

Notice that a new document does not have a ruler bar.

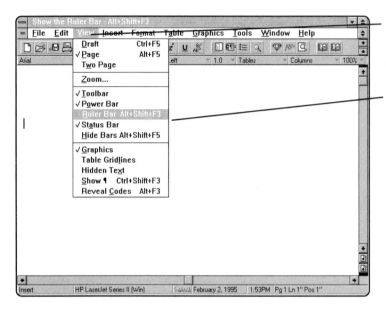

1. **Click** on **View** in the menu bar. A pull-down menu will appear.

2. **Click** on **Ruler Bar**. The ruler bar will appear.

3. **Place** the **mouse pointer** anywhere on the **lower half** of the ruler bar.

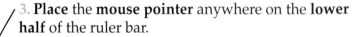

4. **Click** the *right* **mouse button**. A QuickMenu will appear as you see in this example.

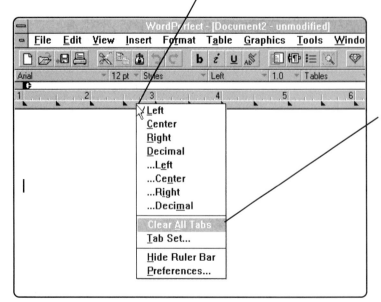

5. **Click** on **Clear All Tabs**. All the tabs on the ruler will disappear.

6. **Place** the **mouse pointer** anywhere on the **lower half** of the ruler bar.

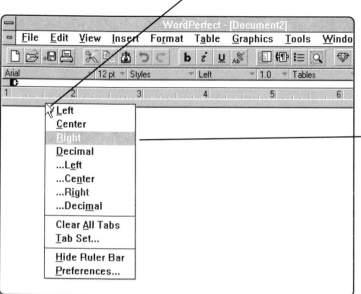

7. **Click** the *right* **mouse button**. A QuickMenu will appear as you see in this example.

8. **Click** on **Right**. The QuickMenu will close, and the tab setting will remain as Right until you change it.

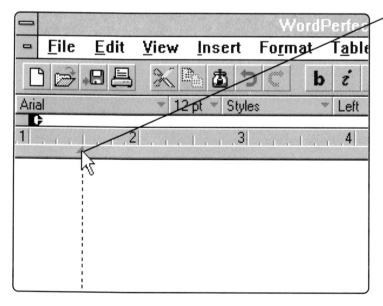

9. **Place** the **mouse arrow** at the **1$^1/_2$ inch mark** on the ruler bar, and **click** to set the tab. You will see a dotted line appear as you hold down the mouse button. A right-aligned tab mark will appear at the 1$^1/_2$ inch mark.

SETTING A
CENTER-ALIGNED TAB

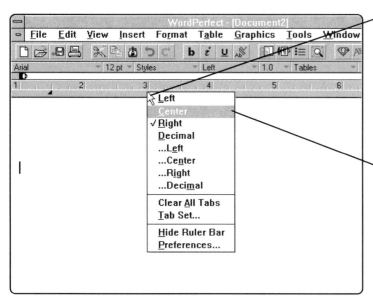

1. **Place** the **mouse pointer** anywhere on the **lower half** of the ruler.

2. **Click** the *right* **mouse button**. A QuickMenu will appear.

3. **Click** on **Center**. The QuickMenu will close, and the tab setting will remain as Center until you change it.

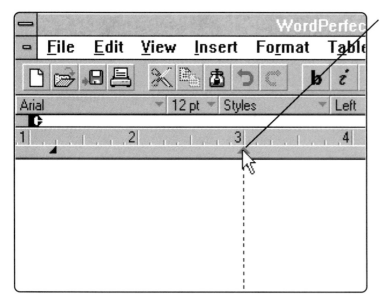

4. **Place** the **mouse pointer** at the **3-inch mark** on the ruler, and **click** to set the tab. A center-aligned tab mark will appear in the ruler bar.

SETTING DECIMAL TABS

In this section you will set two decimal tabs. First, you will change the tab setting to decimal tabs.

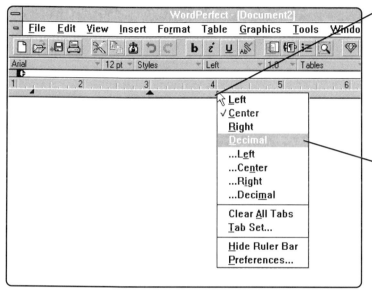

1. **Place** the **mouse button** anywhere on the **lower half** of the ruler bar.

2. **Click** the *right* **mouse button**. A QuickMenu will appear.

3. **Click** on **Decimal**. The QuickMenu will close, and the tab setting will remain as Decimal until you change it.

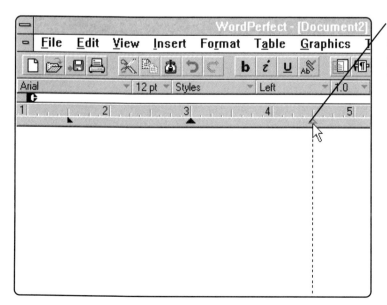

4. **Place** the **mouse pointer** at the **4 ¹/₂ inch mark** on the ruler bar, and click to set the tab.

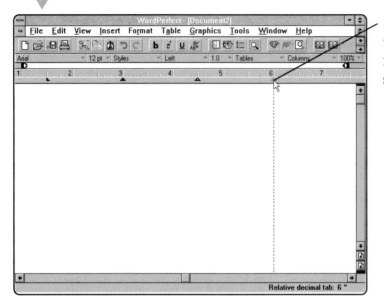

5. **Place** the **mouse arrow** at the **6-inch mark** on the ruler bar, and **click** to set a second decimal tab.

CHANGING LINE SPACING

In this section you will change the line spacing from single to double.

1. **Click** on **Format** on the menu bar. A pull-down list will appear.

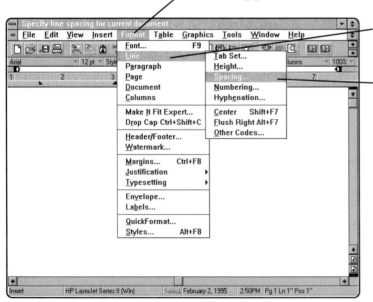

2. **Click** on **Line**. A second menu will appear.

3. **Click** on **Spacing**. The Line Spacing dialog box will appear.

4. **Type 2**. It will replace the highlighted number in the Spacing text box.

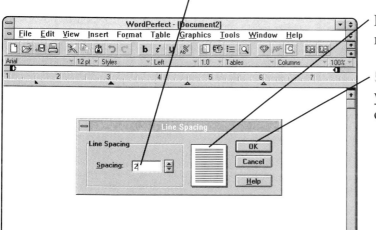

Notice that the Preview reflects the change.

5. **Click** on **OK**. The text in your document will now be double spaced.

APPLYING TABS

In this section you will apply the tabs you set in the previous sections. As you follow these steps, you will see how each text entry aligns on the tabs you set.

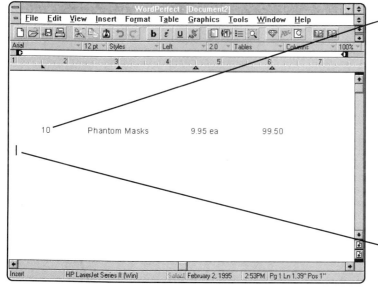

1. **Press Tab** and **type 10**.

2. **Press Tab** and **type Phantom Masks**. Notice that the text moves backwards as you type.

3. **Press Tab** and **type 9.95 ea.**

4. **Press Tab** and **type 99.50**.

5. **Press Enter** once to move down **two lines**.

6. **Press Tab** and **type 5**. Notice that the "5" is right-aligned under "10."

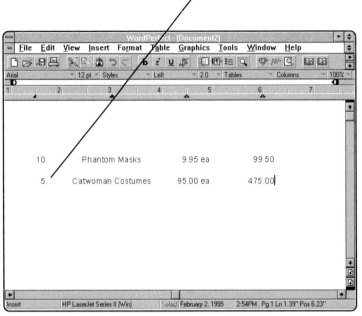

7. **Press Tab** and **type Catwoman Costumes**. Notice that it's centered under the entry above it.

8. **Press Tab** and **type 95.00 ea**. Notice that the decimal points are in line.

9. **Press Tab** and **type 475.00**. Again, notice the decimal points are aligned.

SWITCHING BETWEEN OPEN DOCUMENTS

In this section you will switch back and forth between the unnamed file on your screen and preview.wpd.

1. **Click** on **Window** in the menu bar. A pull-down menu will appear.

2. **Click** on **c:\...\preview.wpd**. (On our computer we installed WordPerfect on the D drive so the filename reads "d:\...\preview.wpd" in this example.) The pull-down menu will disappear, and preview.wpd will be on your screen.

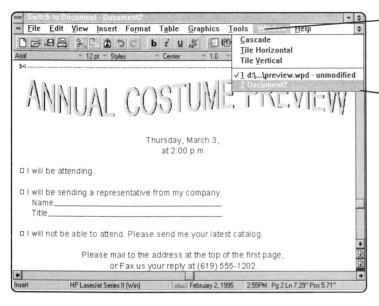

3. **Click** on **Window** in the menu bar. A pull-down menu will appear.

4. **Click** on **Document2**. The pull-down menu will disappear, and the document with the tabs will be on your screen.

CLOSING WITHOUT SAVING

Since the previous tab examples were meant only as practice in setting different types of tabs and will not be used later in the book, you don't need to save the document.

1. **Click** on **File** in the menu bar. A pull-down menu will appear.

2. **Click** on **Close**. A dialog box will appear.

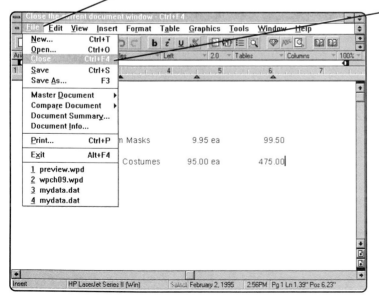

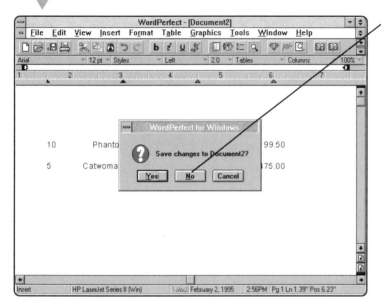

3. **Click** on **No**. The file will close without being saved. Since you never saved this document to begin with, it will simply disappear.

Closing without saving is a handy trick to remember if you have made changes to your document that you don't like. Closing without saving will cause a previously saved document to revert to what it was the last time you saved it.

REMOVING THE RULER BAR

The ruler is useful for doing tasks such as setting tabs. However, it takes up quite a bit of your screen space. For this reason we recommend you remove it when you're not using it.

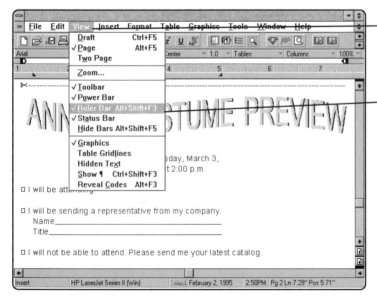

1. **Click** on **View** in the menu bar. A pull-down menu will appear.

2. **Click** on **Ruler Bar**. The pull-down menu will disappear, and the ruler bar will no longer be visible on your screen.

Adding a Header and a Page Number

A header (or footer) is information that is printed at the top (or bottom) of a page. For example, in this book the page number and book title is a header on every left page and the chapter number, title, and page number is a header on every right page. In this chapter, you will do the following:

✔ Change the margin on page 2 of the preview.wpd letter
✔ Insert a header on page 2
✔ Insert a page number on page 2

CHANGING THE MARGIN

In WordPerfect you can change margins as many times as you want within a document. Each time you make a change, the new margin applies to the rest of the document until you change it again. In this section, you will change the top margin on the second page to make space for a header. First, you must go to the top of the page on which you want to make the change.

1. **Press and hold** the **scroll button** and **drag** it up the scroll bar until you can see the page break at the top of page two as you see in this example.

WordPerfect - [c:\...\preview.wpd - unmodified]

File   Edit   View   Insert   Format   Table   Graphics   Tools   Window   Help

Arial   12 pt   Styles   Center   1.0   Tables   Columns   100%

Please return a copy of the form below by Wednesday, February 23.

Sincerely,

Aaron J. Parsons
Vice President

Insert   HP LaserJet 4 (WP)   Select February 1, 1995   2:03PM Pg 2 Ln 7.12" Pos 5.7"

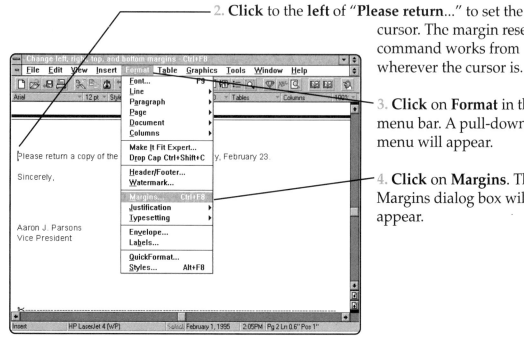

2. **Click** to the **left** of "**Please return**..." to set the cursor. The margin reset command works from wherever the cursor is.

3. **Click** on **Format** in the menu bar. A pull-down menu will appear.

4. **Click** on **Margins**. The Margins dialog box will appear.

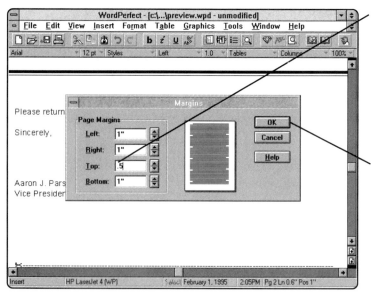

5. **Click twice** in the **Top box. The** "0.600" will be highlighted.

6. **Type .5** to make the top margin on the second page one-half inch.

7. **Click** on **OK**. The document screen will appear with the second page now having a .5 inch top margin.

ADDING A HEADER

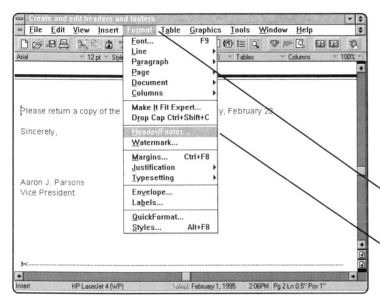

In this section you will create a header for page 2 using the words "Ms. Diane Henderson" and the date.

1. **Click** at the **top** of **page 2** if your cursor is not already there.

2. **Click** on **Format**. A pull-down menu will appear.

3. **Click** on **Header/Footer**. The Headers/Footers dialog box will appear.

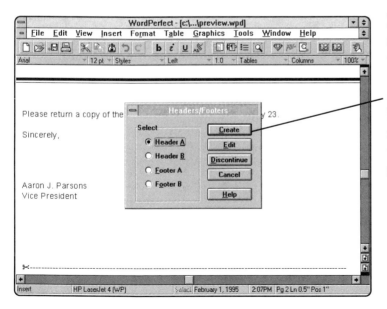

Notice that Header A is already selected (has a dot in the circle).

4. **Click** on **Create**. You will be returned to your document screen, and the header toolbar will appear on your screen below the power bar.

5. **Type Ms. Diane Henderson**.

6. **Press** the **Enter key**.

7. **Type January 12, 1995**.

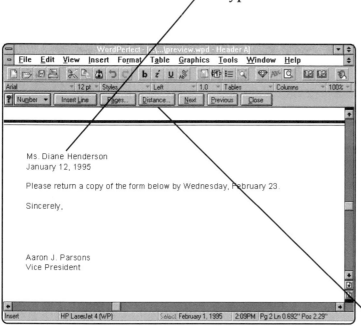

Changing the Distance Between the Header and the Letter

In this section, you'll put a little more space between the header and the letter.

1. **Click** on the **Distance button**. The Distance dialog box will appear.

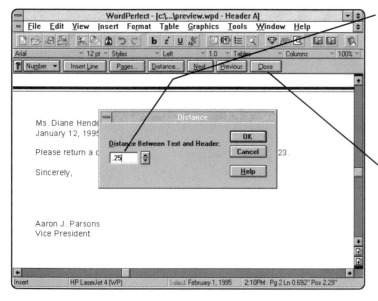

2. **Type .25**. It will replace the highlighted number.

3. **Click** on **OK**. The distance between your header and the first line of text on page 2 will increase to .25".

4. **Click** on **Close** to close the header toolbar.

INSERTING A PAGE NUMBER

To insert a page number, the cursor must be on the page where you want the page numbering to begin.

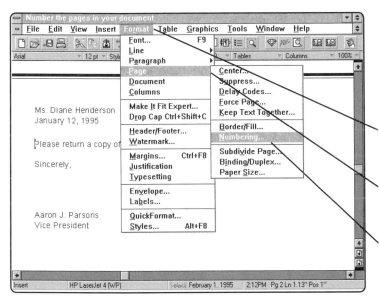

1. **Click next to "Please return"** to place the cursor at the top of page 2 and make sure you are not in the header.

2. **Click** on **Format**. A pull-down menu will appear.

3. **Click** on **Page**. A second menu will appear.

4. **Click** on **Numbering**. The Page Numbering dialog box will appear.

5. **Click and hold** on **No Page Numbering**.

6. **Drag** the **highlight bar down** to **Bottom Center**.

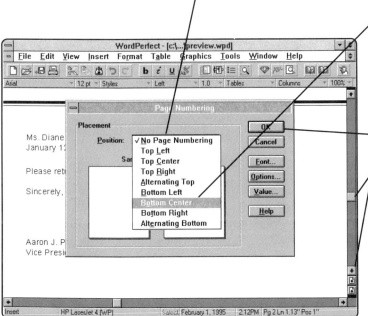

7. **Release** the **mouse button**.

8. **Click** on **OK**.

9. To see the page number, **drag** the **scroll button** to the **bottom** of the **scroll bar**. The page number will be visible.

10. **Click** on the **Save button** to save changes.

Changing the View

Thus far in this book you've been working in the Page view, which is the standard, or default, view in WordPerfect 6.1. This is one of the best views for everyday work. You can, however, change the view of your document so you can see two pages on your screen at the same time or zoom out for a bird's-eye view. In this chapter, you will do the following:

✔ Show two pages at a time
✔ Switch to draft view
✔ Switch to a zoom view

SHOWING TWO PAGES ON THE SCREEN

You can see a bird's-eye of view of both pages at the same time in the Two Page view.

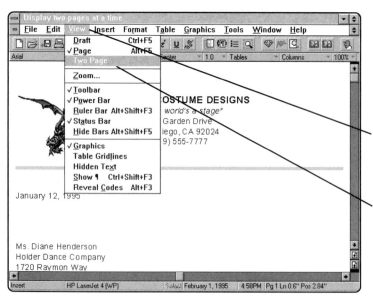

1. **Press and hold** the **Ctrl key** and **press** the **Home key** (Ctrl + Home) to go to the top of the file if you are not already there.

2. **Click** on **View** in the menu bar. A pull-down menu will appear.

3. **Click** on **Two Page**. Your screen will change to show both pages of the letter.

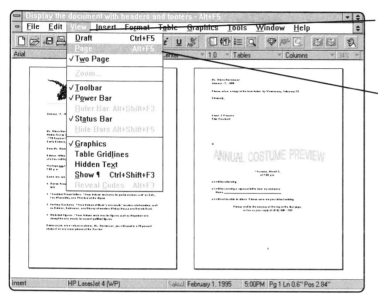

4. **Click** on **View** in the menu bar. A pull-down menu will appear.

5. **Click** on **Page** to return to Page view.

Use the Two Page view before printing to give you an overview of what the document will look like when printed.

SWITCHING TO DRAFT VIEW

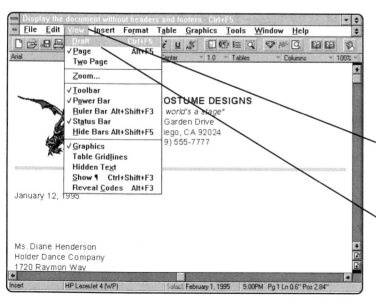

The Draft view is faster to work in because the display is not as good as Page view. Also, you don't see headers, footers, or page numbers in Draft view.

1. **Click** on **View** in the menu bar. A pull-down menu will appear.

2. **Click** on **Draft**. The screen will switch to Draft view.

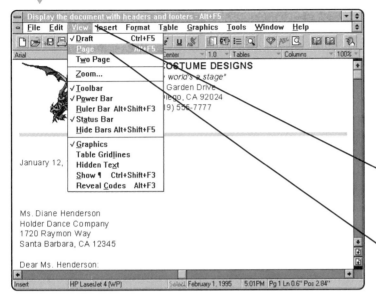

Notice that there's not a great deal of difference in your screen. If you scroll through the document, however, you'll notice that you can't see the header and page number.

3. **Click** on **View** in the menu bar. A pull-down menu will appear.

4. **Click** on **Page** to switch back to the Page view.

ZOOMING OUT

There's a button in the toolbar that will give you a bird's-eye view of the page where your cursor is located.

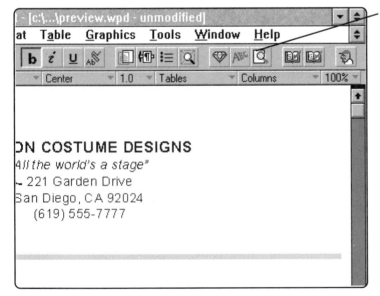

1. **Click** on the **Page/Zoom button** in the toolbar. Your screen will switch to a bird's eye view of the page.

Notice that the Page/Zoom button appears pressed in when this feature is being used.

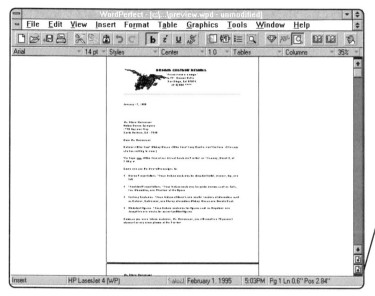

Using the Page Up/Page Down Buttons

No matter what view you're in, you can use the Page Up and Page Down buttons to move through your document.

1. **Click** on the **Page Down button**. It's the bottom button on the scroll bar. You'll move to the next page.

2. **Click** on the **Page Up button** to go up one page. In this example, you'll return to page 1. The Page Up button is the second button from the bottom of the scroll bar.

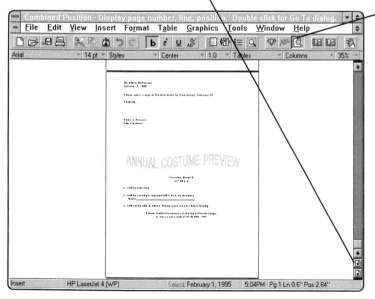

3. **Click** on the **Page/Zoom button** again.

The Page/Zoom view is another way to get an overview of how the document will look before you print it.

CHAPTER

13

Printing an Envelope

Printing an envelope has never been easier! In this chapter, you will do the following:

✔ Print an envelope with and without a return address
✔ Create a list of mailing addresses and return addresses
✔ Change the font on the return address
✔ Change the size of the envelope and the position of the text

OPENING THE ENVELOPE DIALOG BOX

You can print an envelope whether or not you have a letter on your screen. In this example, the Preview letter is open.

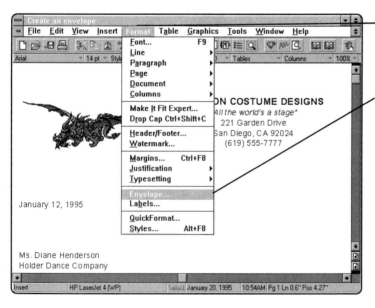

1. **Click** on **Format** in the menu bar. A pull-down menu will appear.

2. **Click** on **Envelope**. The Envelope dialog box will appear.

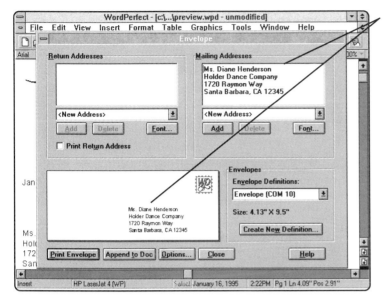

If you open the Envelope dialog box while you have a letter on your screen, WordPerfect will automatically insert the mailing address into the envelope template. (Pretty clever, these WordPerfect programmers!)

ADDING A RETURN ADDRESS

You can save money on preprinted envelopes by adding a return address to the envelope in WordPerfect.

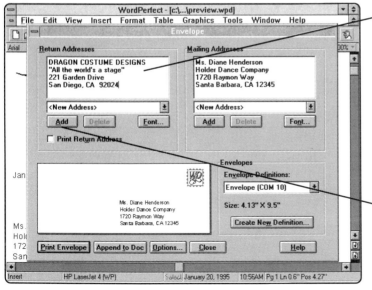

1. **Click inside** the **Return Addresses** box to place the cursor.

2. **Type** your **return address**. Press the Enter key after each line. The envelope sample will flicker as you type.

3. **Click** on **Add**. The first line of the return address will appear in place of <New Address> above the Add button.

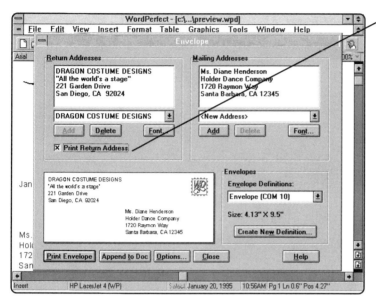

4. **Click** on **Print Return Address** to put an ✕ in the box if one is not there already. The return address will appear on the sample envelope as you see in this example. Even though there is an address in the Return Addresses box, it will not print unless there is an ✕ in this box. You can stop the return address from printing on an envelope by clicking on Print Return Address to *remove* the ✕.

PRINTING

The exact steps you take to print an envelope depend on your printer and whether you have an envelope feeder or whether you must feed individual envelopes by hand. Consult your printer manual for the precise process.

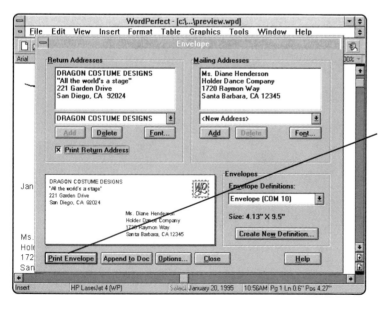

1. **Put** an **envelope** in your printer.

2. **Click** on **Print Envelope**. After a brief pause, you'll see the printing message in the next example.

Depending on your printer, you may have to push a Form Feed button or manually insert an envelope into the feeder. If you have an automatic envelope feeder, you can sit back and relax.

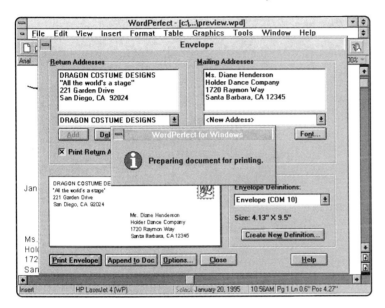

The Envelope dialog box will close after you print.

As you see, printing a standard envelope is a piece of cake. Read on to learn how to customize the envelope. You can even create a library of return addresses and mailing addresses.

CREATING A LIST OF MAILING ADDRESSES

WordPerfect has a really neat feature that allows you to create a list of frequently used names and addresses in the Envelope dialog box. You don't have to have a letter to a person on your screen in order to print an envelope for the person. You can simply select that person's name from the list, and the address will appear on the envelope model.

The following examples show the Preview letter on the screen. However, you can print and customize an envelope without having a letter on your screen.

Adding the Current Address to the Mailing List

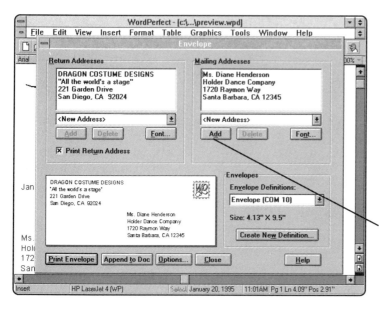

1. **Repeat steps 1 and 2** at the beginning of this chapter to open the Envelope dialog box.

Because the Preview letter is on the screen, Diane Henderson's address shows in the Mailing Addresses box.

2. **Click** on **Add** to add this address to the list. The first line of the address will replace <New Address> above the Add button.

Adding a New Address to the Mailing List

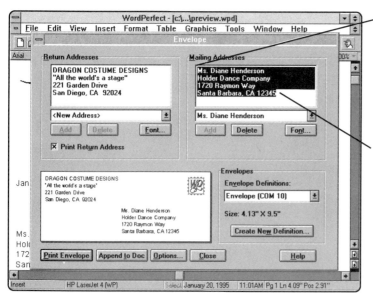

1. If there is an address in the Mailing Addresses box, **click** at the **beginning** of the address to place the cursor. If there is no address, go directly to step 3.

2. **Press and hold** the **mouse button** and **drag** the **cursor** to the end of the line and then down to the end of the address. The entire address will be highlighted as you see in this example.

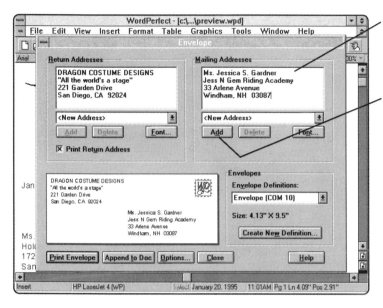

3. **Type** the **new address**. It will replace the highlighted address.

4. **Click** on **Add**. The first line of the address will replace <New Address> above the Add button.

Selecting a Name from the Address List

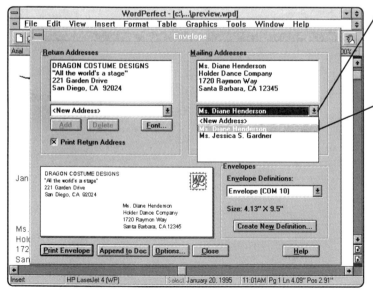

1. **Click** on the ⬇ to the **right** of the address box. A pull-down list of names will appear.

2. **Click** on the **name** you want.

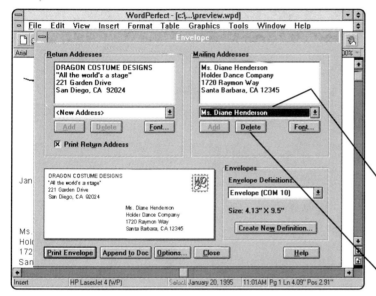

Deleting an Address from the List

You can delete an address from the list if you don't need it any more.

1. **Repeat steps 1 and 2** in the previous section to show the name in the <New Address> box.

2. **Click** on **Delete**. A message box will appear asking if you want to delete the name.

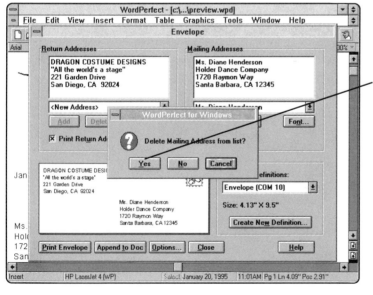

In this example, we'll click on Cancel to cancel the deletion.

3. If you want to delete the name from the list, **Click** on **Yes**.

ADDING A RETURN ADDRESS

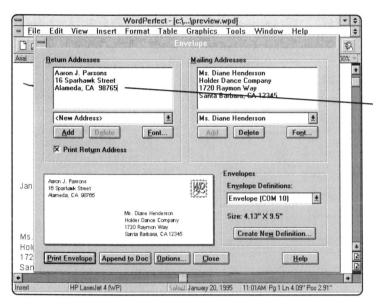

You may want to add a personal return address to the list of return addresses.

1. **Repeat** the steps in "Adding a New Address to the Mailing List" to add a second return address to the list of return addresses.

2. **Repeat** the steps in "Selecting a Name for the Address List" to go back to the return address for Dragon Costume Designs.

CUSTOMIZING THE FONT IN THE RETURN ADDRESS

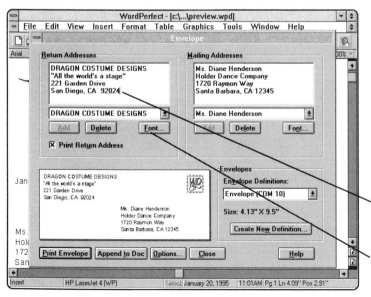

The mailing address and the return address will appear in the font that you selected as your initial font in Chapter 1. You can change the font, but the change applies to all of the lines in the address. You cannot format individual lines in this setup.

1. **Click anywhere** in the Return Addresses box.

2. **Click** on **Font**. The Return Address Font dialog box will appear.

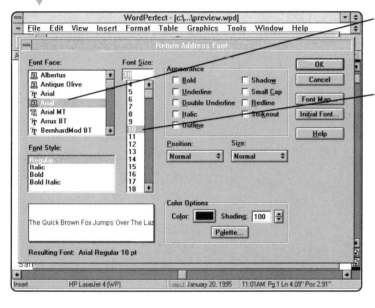

3. **Click** on the **font** you want. In this example, we'll keep the font as Arial.

4. **Click** on the **font size** you want. In this example, click on 10.

These are the only changes we'll make in the font.

5. **Click** on **OK**. The dialog box will close.

CHANGING THE POSITION OF THE ADDRESS ON THE ENVELOPE

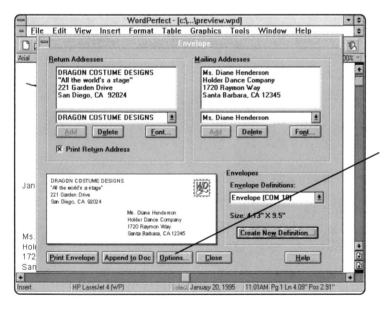

If you don't like the position in which the address (or the return address) prints, you can make it print higher, lower, or more to the right or left.

1. **Click** on **Options**. The Envelope Options dialog box will appear.

2. Click twice in the **Vertical Position box**. The number will be highlighted. This number controls the placement of the address from the top edge of the envelope.

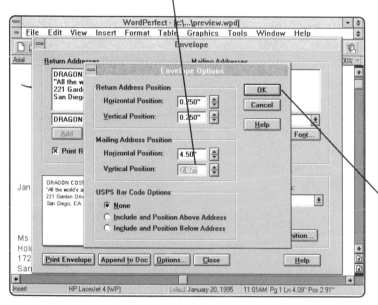

3. Type the **new measurement**. Type a larger number to lower the address on the envelope. Type a smaller number to raise the address on the envelope. In this example, we won't change the position of the address on the envelope.

4. Click on **OK** to close the Envelope Options dialog box. You'll be back at the Envelope dialog box.

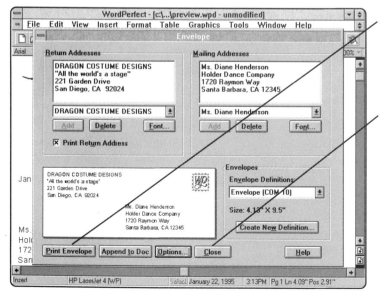

5a. Click on **Print Envelope** to print the envelope again.

Or,

5b. Click on **Close** to close the dialog box without printing the envelope.

Creating a Mailing List

With the WordPerfect 6.1 Merge feature, you can send the same letter to different people and have the individual's name, address, salutation, and other information personalized on each letter without having to retype each letter. If you're following along with this book, you typed the letter in Parts I and II. In this chapter, you will do the following:

✔ Create a data entry table
✔ Create a mailing list

CLOSING OPEN FILES

You can create a mailing list when there is a document on your screen. However, the examples in this chapter will begin with an empty screen.

1. **Click twice** on the **Control menu box** of the preview document if it is on your screen. If you saved the letter just prior to clicking on the Control menu box, the letter will simply close. If you didn't save it, a message box will appear asking if you want to save changes in the file.

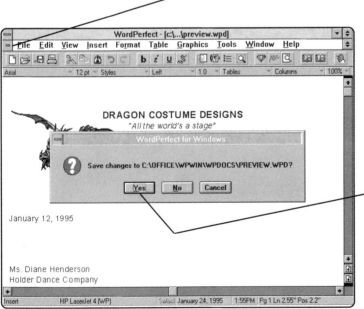

2. **Click** on **Yes** to save any changes. The letter will close, and you'll have a blank WordPerfect screen.

SETTING UP A MAILING LIST

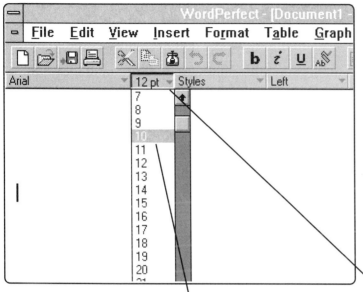

We think the easiest way to create a mailing list is to enter the information into a table, called a *data entry table*. Typing with a smaller font allows you to see more of the table on your screen, but it will not change the font you select for the printed letter.

Changing Font Size

1. **Click** on the ▼ to the **right** of the **font size**. A pull-down list of font sizes will appear.

2. **Click** on **10** to change the font for this specific document to 10 points.

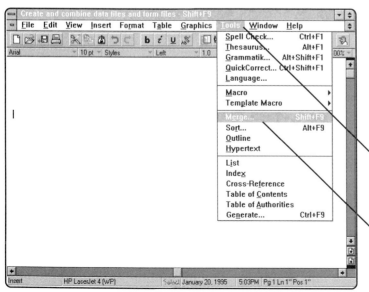

Opening a Data Table

In this section you'll create a table to hold your mailing list information.

1. **Click** on **Tools** in the menu bar. A pull-down menu will appear.

2. **Click** on **Merge**. The Merge dialog box will appear.

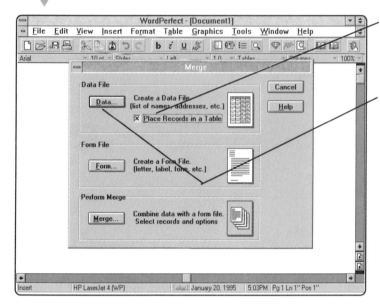

3. **Click** on **Place Records in a Table** to put an X in the box.

4. **Click** on **Data**. The Create Merge File dialog box will appear.

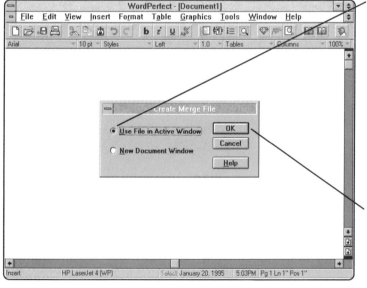

5. **Click** on **Use File in Active Window** to put a dot in the circle if one is not already there.

Note: If you start a data file with another document on your screen, click on New Document Window to open a new file.

6. **Click** on **OK**. The Create Merge File dialog box will appear.

CREATING A MAILING LIST

In a mailing list, information is broken into fields such as last name, first name, street, city, etc. When you create a mailing list in table form, each field goes in its own column in the table. Each column has a heading, called a *field name*, that identifies the kind of information in the field. You don't have to type the field names in upper case letters as shown in the examples in this section. However, the field names will become headings in the table and will stand out better if they are in upper case letters.

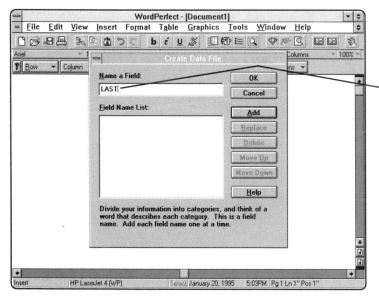

1. **Press** the **Caps Lock key** on your keyboard to turn on the capital letter function.

2. **Type** the word **LAST** in the Name a Field text box.

3. **Press** the **Enter key** (or click on Add). "LAST" will move to the Field Name List box below.

Warning: Do **not** click on OK. If you do, the Quick Data Entry screen you see on page 147 will appear. If that happens, do this:

✔ **Click** on **Close** in the Quick Data Entry screen. A message box will appear asking if you want to save changes to disk.
✔ **Click** on **No** in the message box.
✔ **Click** on **File** in the menu bar.
✔ **Click** on **Close**. A message box will appear asking if you want to save changes to the document.
✔ **Click** on **No** in the message box.
✔ **Start over again** with "Changing Font Size"!

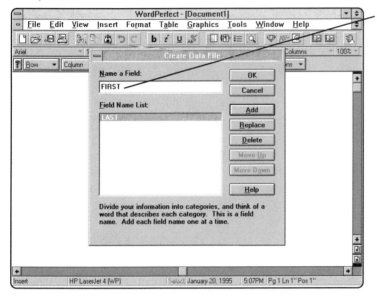

4. **Type** the word **FIRST** in the Name a Field box.

5. **Press** the **Enter key.** "FIRST" will move down to the Field Name List box under LAST.

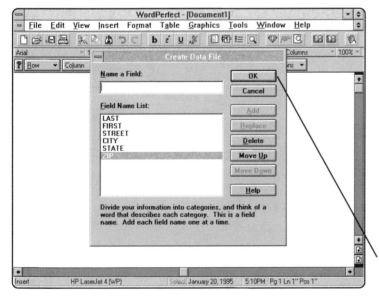

6. **Repeat steps 4 and 5** to enter the following words (field names) in the Name a Field text box:

STREET

CITY

STATE

ZIP

7. **Click** on **OK.** The Quick Data Entry dialog box will appear.

ENTERING DATA IN A MAILING LIST WITH QUICK DATA ENTRY

There are two ways to enter data in a list. In this example you will use a dialog box.

Notice that the cursor is flashing in the LAST field box.

1. **Type Feldman**. (Make sure you have pressed the Caps Lock key to turn the capital letters function off. If you forgot, simply press the Backspace key to erase FELDMAN and type the word again.)

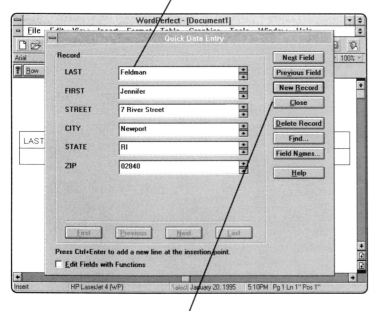

2. **Press** the **Enter key** (or the Tab key) to move to the next box.

3. **Type** the appropriate entry in the FIRST, STREET, CITY, STATE, and ZIP boxes respectively. (Remember to press Enter after each entry.)

If you were going to enter another record or name, using the Quick Data Entry dialog box, you would click on New Record. In this example, you will enter just this one record for Jennifer Feldman.

4. **Click** on **Close**. The Quick Data Entry dialog box will close, and WordPerfect will ask if you want to save the changes you have made.

Saving a Mailing List

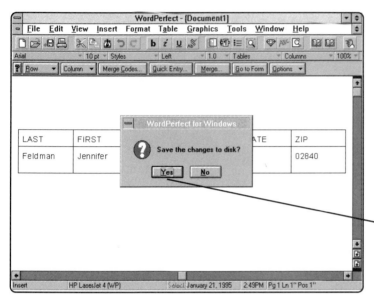

When you close the Quick Data Entry dialog box, WordPerfect will ask if you want to save the changes to disk. (Don't worry about the "saving to disk" part. It's just computer talk for saving. Don't you wish they'd say it in plain English?)

1. **Click** on **Yes**. Because you haven't named the file, the Save Data File As dialog box will appear.

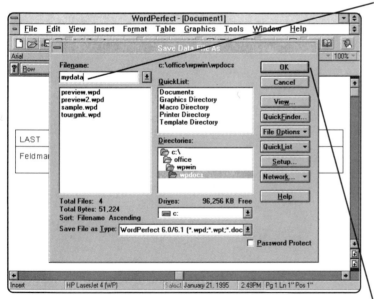

2. **Type** a **name** for the list. In this example, it is mydata. The name should have no more than eight letters. The new name will replace the highlighted *.* that is in the Filename box when this dialog box appears on your screen.

Notice that this file will be saved in the wpdocs subdirectory under wpwin, which is in the office directory.

3. **Click** on **OK**. This dialog box will close, and a table will be on your screen with Jennifer Feldman's information.

ENTERING DATA DIRECTLY INTO A MAILING LIST TABLE

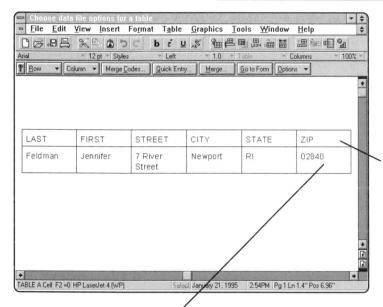

In the previous section you used the Quick Data Entry dialog box to enter data into the mailing list table. In this section you will enter data directly into the table.

Notice that the first row of the table contains the field names. This row is called the *header row*.

Adding a Blank Row to the Table

1. While the cursor is in the last cell of the table, **press the Tab key**. This will add a blank row to the table. The cursor will be flashing in the first cell of the new line.

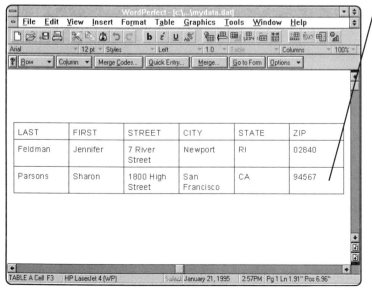

2. **Type** the following five fields in the table. **Press** the **Tab key** to move to each new cell:

Parsons
Sharon
1800 High Street
San Francisco
CA
94567

SAVING CHANGES
TO A MAILING LIST

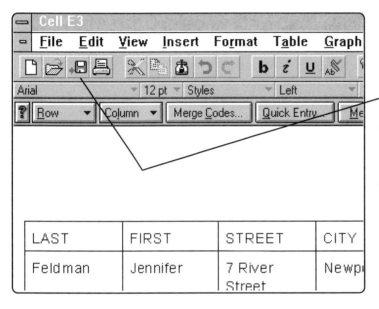

Now that you have added a record to the data list, you'll want to save the list again.

1. **Click** on the **Save button** on the toolbar. It's the third button from the left. Because you have already named the file, the changes will simply be saved.

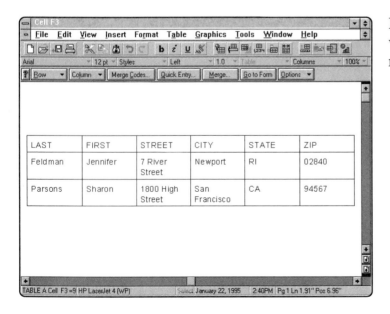

If you plan to follow along with the next chapter, do not exit the file.

CHAPTER 15

Editing a Mailing List

Suppose you created and saved a mailing list, as you did in Chapter 14, and then discovered that you didn't include fields for a company name and a person's title, for example. In WordPerfect 6.1 it's easy to make changes and additions to your mailing list. In this chapter, you will do the following:

✔ Add fields to the mailing list
✔ Add data into the new fields
✔ Add a new record to the mailing list
✔ Save the mailing list

ADDING FIELDS TO THE MAILING LIST

In this section you will add two field headings to the data entry table, one for PREFIX and one for COMPANY.

1. **Open** the **MYDATA** file that you created in Chapter 14 if it's not already open.

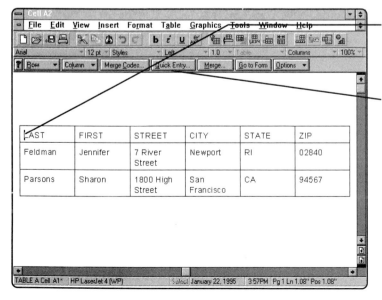

2. **Click** on the **first cell** in the table to place the cursor to the left of LAST.

3. **Click** on **Quick Entry** in the feature bar. The Quick Data Entry dialog box will appear. (Notice that this special feature bar appears automatically when you open a data file.)

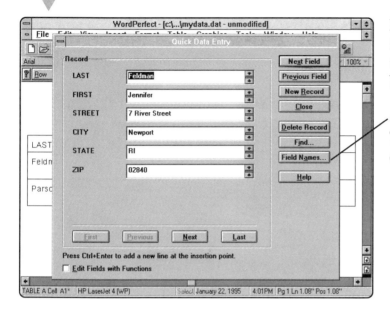

Notice that the fields and first record of the mydata table appear in the dialog box.

4. **Click** on **Field Names**. The Edit Field Names dialog box will appear.

Notice that the cursor is flashing in the Field Name text box.

5. **Type PREFIX** (in capital letters) in the Field Name text box.

6. **Click** on **Add Before**. PREFIX will be added to the top of the list of Field Names.

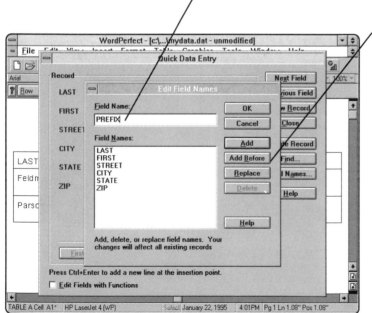

Adding a Field Name to the Middle of the List

1. **Click** on **STREET** in the Field Names text box to highlight it.

Notice that STREET automatically appears in the Field Name text box.

2. **Click twice** on **STREET** to highlight it.

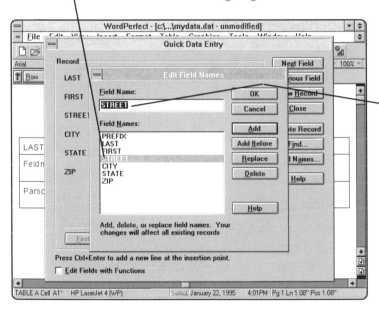

3. **Type COMPANY**. It will replace STREET.

4. **Click** on **Add Before**. COMPANY will be inserted ahead of STREET, which is the highlighted selection in the list of field names.

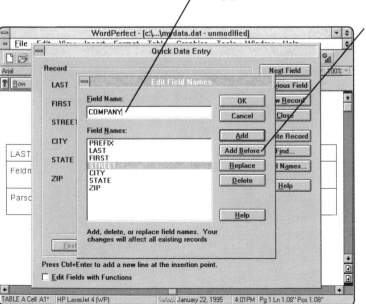

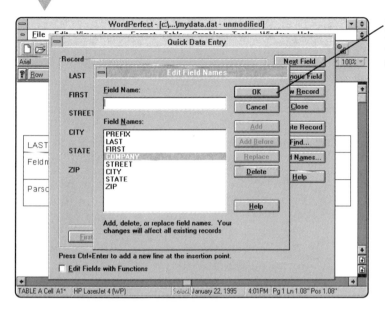

5. **Click** on **OK**. The Quick Data Entry dialog box will appear.

Adding Data into the New Fields

Notice that the cursor is flashing in the PREFIX field.

1. **Type Ms.** in the PREFIX field. (Make sure your Caps Lock function is turned off.)

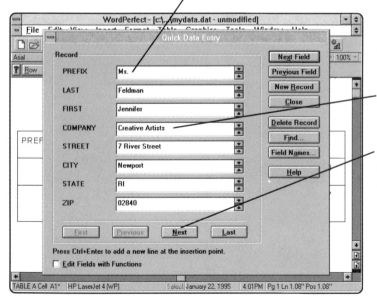

2. **Press** the **Tab key** three times to move to the COMPANY field.

3. **Type Creative Artists** in the COMPANY field.

4. **Click** on **Next**. A second Quick Data Entry screen will appear.

5. **Type Ms.** in the PREFIX field.

6. **Press** the **Tab key** three times to reach the COMPANY field. (Or you can simply click in the field box.)

7. **Type Entertainment Unlimited** in the COMPANY field.

8. **Click** on **Close**. The Save changes to disk message box will appear.

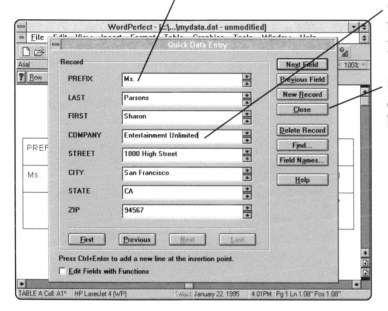

9. **Click** on **Yes**. The Save Data File As dialog box will appear.

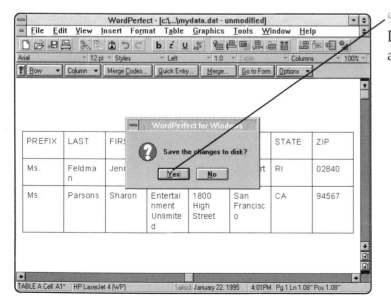

WordPerfect 6.1 is a little paranoid about changes to data files. Every time you make a change to a data file, one of these Save As boxes pops up.

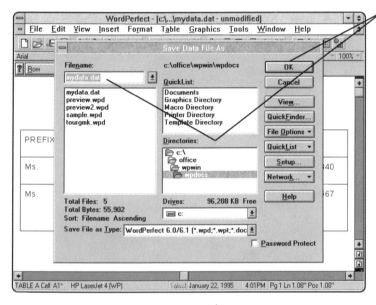

10. Click on **OK**. This will save the file with the same name (mydata.dat) that shows in the Filename box. If you wanted to save this new version as a separate file, you would type a new name in the Filename box. This new version would be saved with the new name and the old version (under the previous name) would remain unchanged.

Because you said you wanted to save this file with the same name, WordPerfect reminds you once again that this filename already exists, and that saving the file with the same name will replace the existing file with this new version. Because that's exactly what you want:

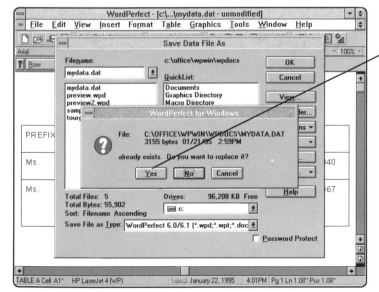

11. Click on **Yes**. The dialog boxes will close, and the edited table will be on your screen.

ADDING A NEW RECORD
TO THE MAILING LIST

It's quick and easy to make additions to a mailing list.

1. **Click** on **Ms.** in the first cell of the table to place the cursor.

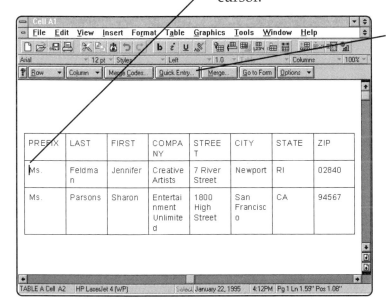

2. **Click** on **Quick Entry.** The Quick Data Entry dialog box will appear.

Notice that the first entry on the mailing list appears. If you had clicked in another row on the table, a different entry would have appeared.

3. **Click** on **New Record**. A second Quick Data Entry screen will appear.

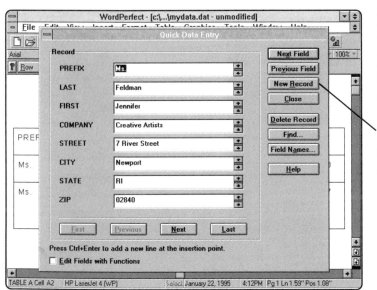

Notice that the cursor is flashing in the PREFIX field.

4. **Type** the appropriate information in the field name boxes.

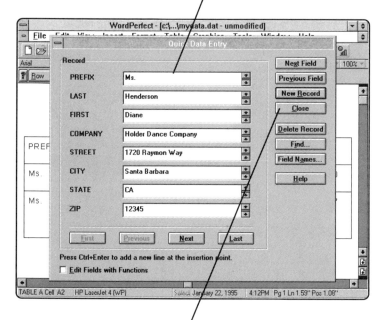

Notice that this example shows the same name that is in the letter you typed in Parts I and II of this book. If you want Diane Henderson to receive a personalized copy of the letter, you must add her name to the mailing list because in the next chapter you'll replace Diane Henderson's information in the original letter with a code that tells WordPerfect to use the information from the mailing list every time it prints the letter.

5. **Click** on **Close.** A Save changes to disk message will appear once again.

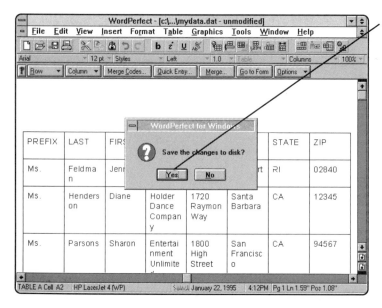

6. **Click** on **Yes.** The Save Data File As dialog box will reappear. (We told you WordPerfect was a little paranoid about these changes.)

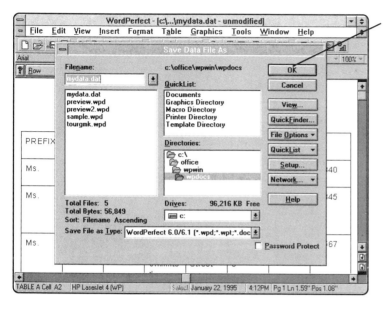

7. **Click** on **OK** to save the file under the same name.

Three guesses as to which dialog box comes up next. You guessed it . . . the message asking if you want to replace the existing file (not shown here).

8. **Click** on **Yes**.

Notice that the columns have become narrower to accommodate the additional two columns (field names) that you added. This causes words to be divided in funny places and placed on separate lines in a box. This will have absolutely no affect on how they print in the merged letter.

However, if it disturbs your sensibilities to look at them, refer to Chapter 20, "Editing a Table" to learn how to change column width.

Also note that you can sort the entries in the table based on the last name so they appear alphabetized. See Chapter 20, "Editing a Table," to learn how to sort.

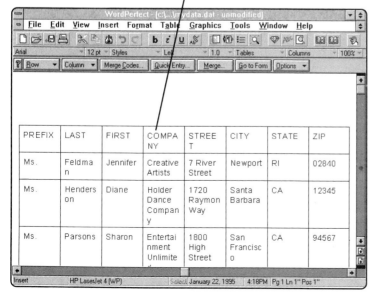

Setting Up
a Form Letter
for Merge Printing

In Chapter 15 you completed your mailing list by adding new fields and data. You are now ready to code the letter to match the mailing list so that it will print personalized letters. In this chapter you will do the following:

✔ Insert merge fields into a form letter

CREATING A FORM LETTER

In this section, you'll tell WordPerfect to use the preview.wpd letter as the form letter.

1. **Open** the **preview.wpd** document that you created in Chapters 1-11.

2. **Click** on **Tools** in the menu bar. A pull-down menu will appear.

3. **Click** on **Merge**. The Merge dialog box will appear.

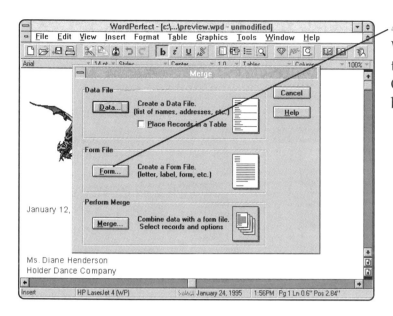

4. **Click** on **Form** to tell WordPerfect that you want to create a form letter. The Create Merge File dialog box will appear.

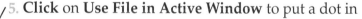

5. **Click** on **Use File in Active Window** to put a dot in the circle if it does not already have one. You are selecting this option because you want to use the preview document that is on your screen. In other words, you want to *use the file in the active window.*

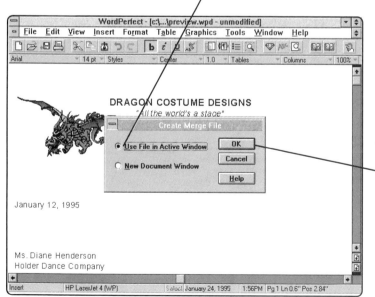

6. **Click** on **OK**. The Create Form File dialog box will appear.

CONNECTING A MAILING LIST TO A FORM LETTER

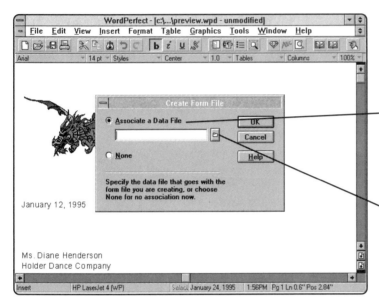

In this section, you'll connect the mailing list that you created in Chapters 14 and 15 to this form letter.

1. **Click** on **Associate a Data File** to place a dot in the circle if it does not already have one.

2. **Click** on the **button** to the **right** of the blank text box. The Select File dialog box will appear.

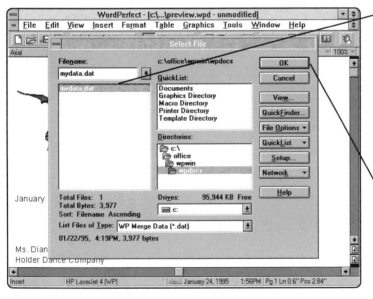

3. **Click** on mydata.dat to highlight it. Notice that WordPerfect recognized that it was a data file from its format and added the ".dat" extension instead of the ".wpd" extension to the filename.

4. **Click** on **OK**. The Create Form File dialog box will appear.

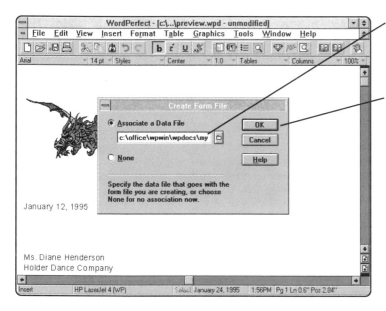

Notice that mydata now appears in the Associate a Data File text box.

5. **Click** on **OK**. The preview document screen will reappear.

INSERTING MERGE FIELDS INTO A FORM LETTER

In this section, you'll erase Diane Henderson's information and replace it with field names from your mailing list.

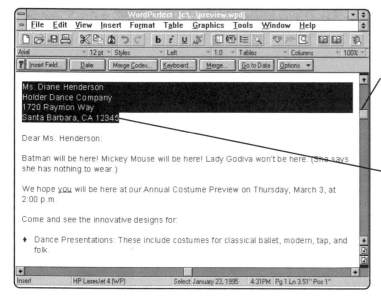

Setting up the Address

1. **Drag** the **scroll bar button** $^{1}/_{4}$ of the way down the scroll bar so that you can see the inside address of the letter.

2. **Click** to the **right** of the **ZIP code** in the mailing address to set the cursor.

3. **Press and hold** the **mouse button** and **drag** it **up** to highlight the entire address, then **release** it.

4. **Press** the **Backspace key** to delete the address. The cursor will be flashing where the word "Ms." was located.

5. **Click** on **Insert Field** in the Merge feature bar. The Insert Field Name or Number dialog box will appear as you see in this example.

Unfortunately, this dialog box picked an inconvenient spot in which to appear because it will get in the way of your seeing the inside address codes. Fortunately, it's easily moved.

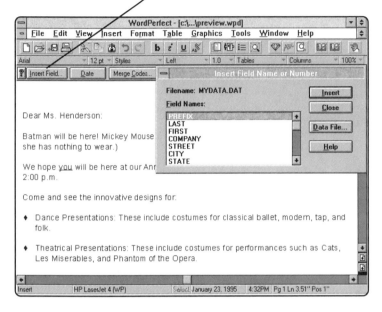

Moving a Dialog Box

You can move any dialog box with these steps.

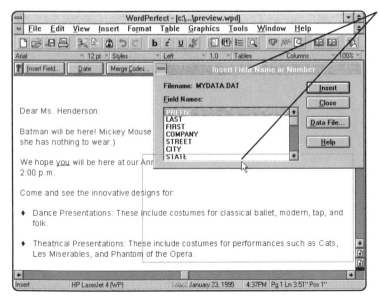

1. **Click and hold** on the **title bar** of the dialog box and **drag** the dialog box to the bottom of the screen. You'll see an outline of the dialog box moving with the mouse pointer.

2. **Release** the **mouse button** when the outline is placed where you want the dialog box to be. When you release the mouse button, the box will appear in place of the outline.

Inserting Field Codes into the Address

In this section, you'll insert the field names from the mailing list into the form letter.

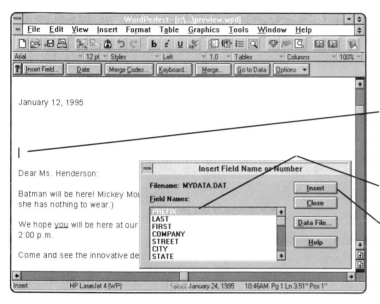

1. **Click** two lines **above "Dear Ms. Henderson"** to place the cursor.

2. **Click** on **PREFIX**.

3. **Click** on **Insert**. FIELD(PREFIX) will appear at the cursor in the first line of the address as you see in the example below.

4. **Press** the **Spacebar once** to put a space after the PREFIX field.

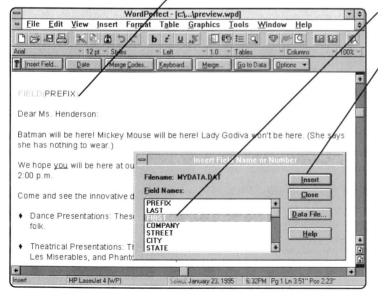

5. **Click** on **FIRST** to highlight it.

6. **Click** on **Insert**. FIELD(FIRST) will appear after FIELD(PREFIX) in the first line of the address.

Note: You don't have to insert field names in the order in which they appear in the Field Name dialog box. You can insert field names in any order, as you did here.

7. **Press** the **Spacebar once** to insert a space after FIELD(FIRST).

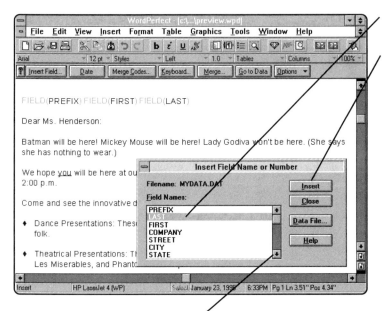

8. **Click** on **LAST**.

9. **Click** on **Insert**.

If you goof and insert the wrong merge field, simply highlight it and delete it. Then repeat steps 8 and 9 to replace it with the correct merge field.

10. **Press** the **Enter key** on your keyboard to move to the next line in the letter.

11. **Click** on the ⬇ to scroll to the bottom of the Select Field Names box so you can see ZIP at the bottom of the list.

12. **Enter** the following words (field names) in the mailing address area of the letter, pressing the Enter key at the end of each line:

COMPANY
STREET
CITY, STATE ZIP

Note: Make sure to insert a comma and a space after FIELD(CITY). Put two spaces between the STATE and ZIP fields.

SETTING UP THE SALUTATION

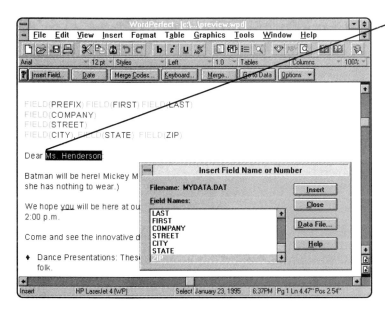

1. **Click** to the **left** of **"Ms. Henderson"** to set the cursor.

2. **Press and hold** the **mouse button** as you **drag** the highlight bar **over Ms. Henderson**. Be careful *not* to highlight the colon.

3. **Press** the **Backspace key** to delete the prefix and name.

4. **Repeat steps 2-4** in the previous section to add the following two fields to the salutation:

PREFIX

LAST

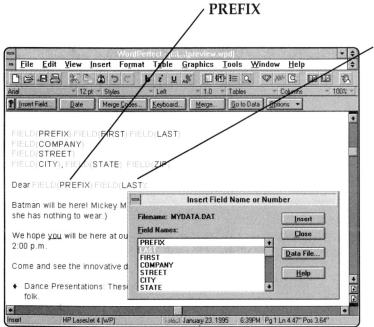

Remember to press the Spacebar between the PREFIX and LAST fields.

SETTING UP THE BODY TEXT

In this section, you'll insert a field code into the body of the letter.

1. **Click repeatedly** on the ⬇ on the scroll bar until you can see the double line indicating the page break.

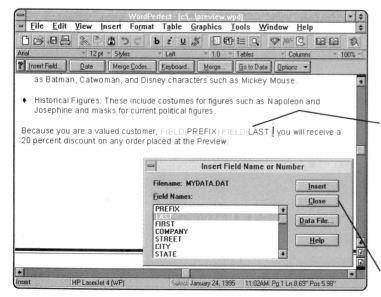

2. **Click** to the **left** of "**Ms. Henderson**" to set the cursor.

3. **Press** and **hold** the **mouse button** as you **drag** it **across the name and prefix**. Do not highlight the comma after the name. **Release** the **mouse button**.

4. **Press** the **Backspace key** to delete the prefix and name.

5. **Repeat** the **steps** in the section "Inserting Field Codes into the Address" to insert the following two fields:

PREFIX LAST

Note: Check the spacing between words carefully. You may have to go back and insert a space after you have inserted a field code.

6. **Click** on **Close**.

COPYING AND
PASTING FIELD CODES

You can use the Copy and Paste buttons to copy the field codes from the mailing address on page 1 to the second page of the letter.

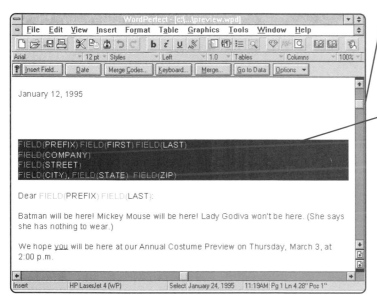

1. **Click and hold** on the **scroll bar button** and **drag** it up so that you can see the inside address field codes.

2. **Click** to the **right** of the **last line** in the mailing address.

3. **Press and hold** the **mouse button** and **drag** the highlight bar **up** over the four lines of code.

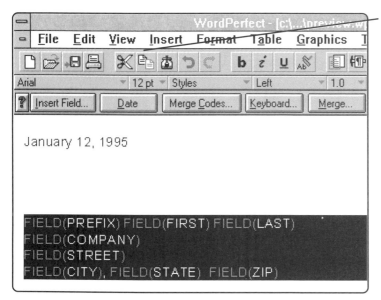

4. **Click** on the **Copy button**. The highlight will disappear from the mailing address lines. These lines are now copied to the Clipboard, a temporary storage area in your computer's memory.

5. Press and hold the **Ctrl key** and **press** the **End key** (Ctrl + End) to go to the end of the file.

6. Click to the **left** of the **first check box** to place the cursor.

7. Click on the **Paste button** in the toolbar. The field codes for the address will be pasted into the letter at the cursor.

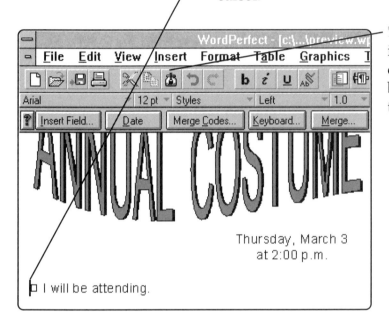

Notice that the cursor is still in front of the first check box, so you'll have to move the check box down a couple of lines.

8. Press the **Enter key twice** to move the check box down two lines on the letter.

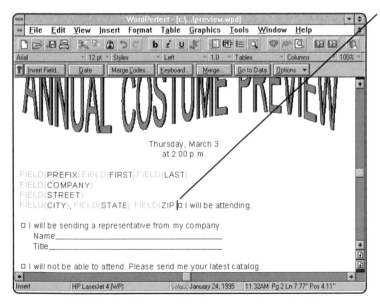

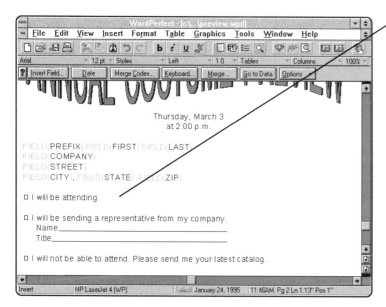

Your letter should look like this example.

INSERTING PERSONALIZED INFORMATION INTO A HEADER

You can put field codes any place in a letter. In this section, you'll personalize the header on page 2.

1. **Click** in the left margin **beside** the **field codes for "Ms. Diane Henderson"** in the address you just pasted onto page 2. The line will be highlighted.

2. **Click** on the **Copy button** in the toolbar to copy the highlighted data.

3. **Click** on the ⬆ on the scroll bar to go up to the top of page 2.

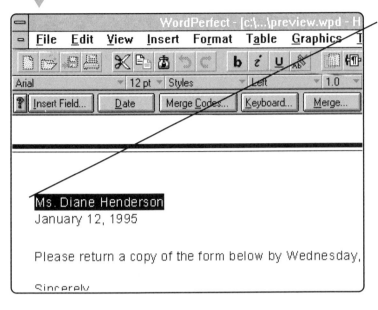

4. **Click** to the **left** of **"Ms. Diane Henderson"** in the header.

5. **Press and hold** the **mouse button** and **drag** the highlight bar over the name.

6. **Click** on the **Paste button** in the toolbar to paste the codes into the header as you see here.

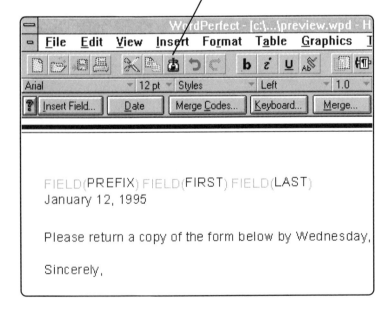

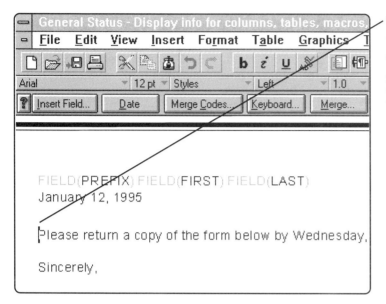

7. **Click** to the **left** of "**Please Return**" to move the cursor out of the header field and back into the letter.

SAVING THE FORM LETTER WITH THE SAVE AS COMMAND

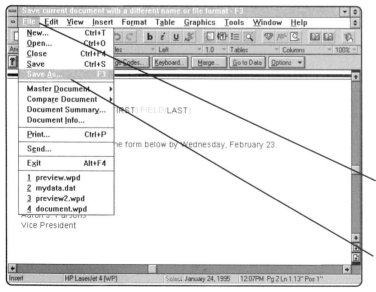

You can keep the original PREVIEW letter unchanged if you use the Save As command. This command allows you to give a new name to the changed version and keep the original letter intact.

1. **Click** on **File** in the menu bar. A pull-down menu will appear.

2. **Click** on **Save As**. The Save As dialog box will appear.

3. **Type myform** in the Filename text box.

4. **Click** on **OK**.

You are now ready to merge print the form letter with the mailing list.

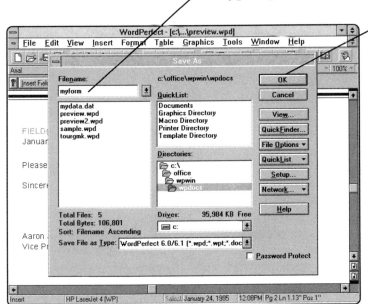

Printing Letters and Envelopes for a Mailing List

Once you have a coded form letter (Chapter 16), you're ready to print it by *merging* the coded letter with the data file (the mailing list). In this chapter, you will do the following:

✔ Merge print letters and envelopes for a mailing list
✔ Merge print a specific letter from a mailing list

SETTING UP TO PRINT A FORM LETTER

You can begin the merge printing process without having any files open on your screen, but it's easier if you have the letter you want to merge on your screen.

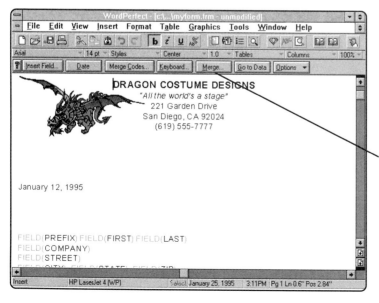

Beginning the Merge Process

1. **Open** the **coded myform letter** if it is not already on your screen.

2. **Click** on the **Merge button** in the special Merge bar. The Merge dialog box will appear.

(You can also click on Tools in the menu bar, then click on Merge on the resulting pull-down menu.)

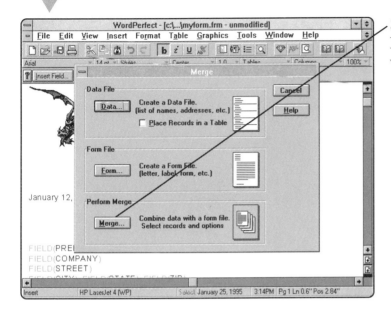

3. **Click** on **Merge**. The Perform Merge dialog box will appear.

SELECTING THE FORM FILE

Because you started the merge process with the coded form letter on your screen, WordPerfect has already identified the appropriate Form File.

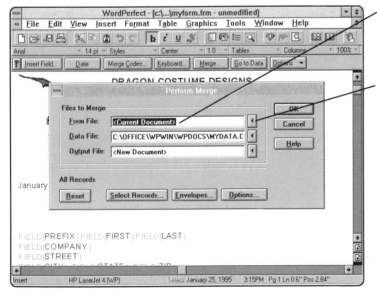

1. **Confirm** that **<Current Document>** is in the Form File box.

Note: If the coded letter is not on your screen, click on the button to the right of the Form File box and select your file.

SELECTING THE DATA FILE

When you start the merge process with the coded form letter on your screen, this step is handled by WordPerfect.

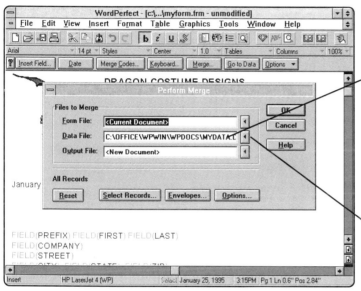

1. Confirm that **mydata.dat** is the file listed in the Data File box. WordPerfect knows which data file to use because you already linked (associated) the letter to a data file.

Note: If the correct data file is not listed here, click on the button to the right and select the correct file.

SELECTING THE PRINTER

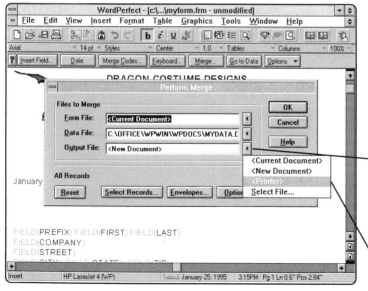

Once you've specified the letter (form file) and the mailing list (data file) as you did in the two preceding sections, you're ready to tell WordPerfect to print the merged letters.

1. Click on the **button** to the **right** of the Output File text box. A menu will appear.

2. Click on **<Printer>**. "Printer" will appear in the Output File text box.

PRINTING ENVELOPES
FOR A MAILING LIST

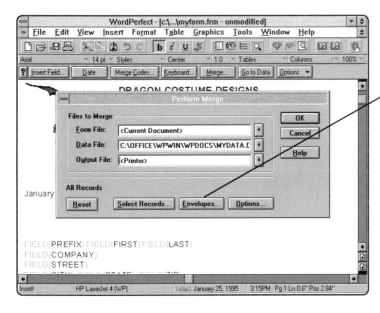

While you are in the Perform Merge dialog box, you can print envelopes.

1. **Click** on **Envelopes**. The Envelope dialog box will appear.

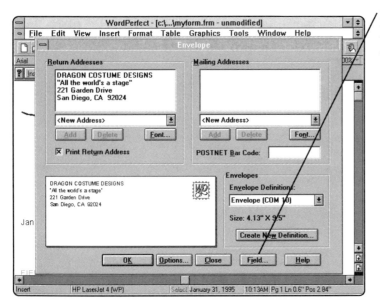

2. **Click** on **Field**. The Insert Field Name or Number dialog box will appear.

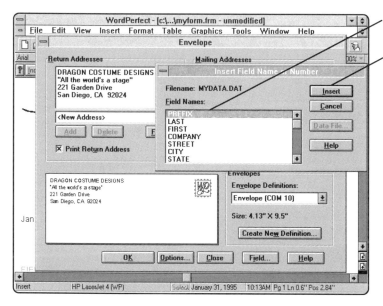

3. **Click** on **PREFIX**.

4. **Click** on **Insert**. Unfortunately, the dialog box closes and you have to open it again.

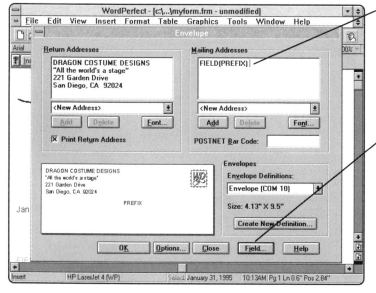

Notice the PREFIX field in the Mailing Addresses box.

5. **Press** the **Spacebar** on your keyboard to put a space after the prefix.

6. **Click** on **Field** again. The Insert Field Name or Number dialog box will appear again.

7. **Continue to repeat steps 3 and 4** to add the fields for the address, as you see in the next example. Remember to put a comma after the city field and two spaces after the state field.

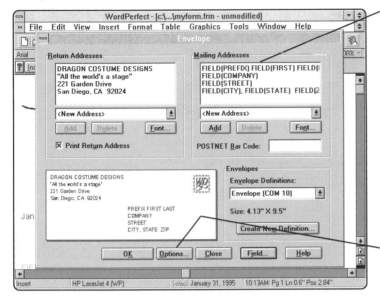

Notice the completed address.

Adding a USPS Bar Code to the Envelope

If you're doing a large mailing, check with the Post Office about the value of adding a bar code.

1. **Click** on **Options**. The Envelope Options dialog box will appear.

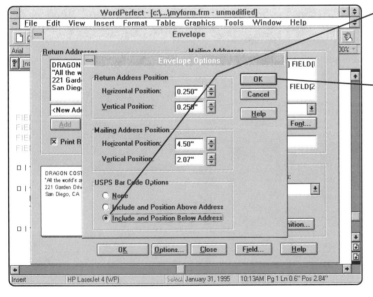

2. **Click** on **Include and Position Below Address** to put a dot in the circle.

3. **Click** on **OK**. This tells WordPerfect where to print the bar code. In a regular (non-merged) envelope, the bar code will appear on the sample envelope in the Envelope dialog box. Because this is an envelope for a merged file, you must merge the ZIP code into the POSTNET Bar Code box.

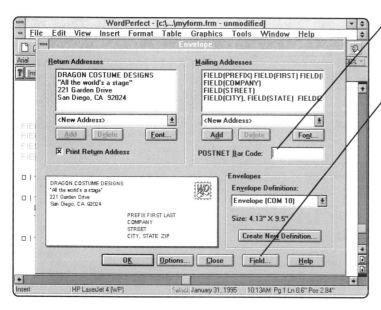

4. **Click** in the **POSTNET Bar Code box** to place the cursor.

5. **Click** on **Field** (yet again). The Insert Field Name or Number dialog box will appear. Don't you wish this silly box would just stay open the way it does when you code the letter?

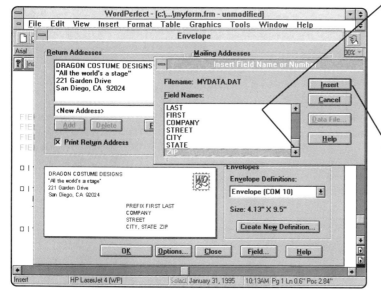

6. **Click** on the ⬇ to scroll down the Field Names list so you can see ZIP.

7. **Click** on **ZIP** to highlight it.

8. **Click** on **Insert**. ZIP will be inserted into the POSTNET Bar Code box.

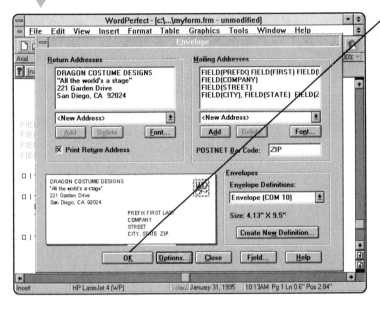

9. **Click** on **OK**. The Envelope dialog box will close and you'll be back at the Perform Merge dialog box that you see below.

MERGE PRINTING LETTERS AND ENVELOPES

All the preparation is now done, and you're ready to actually print. Hurrah!

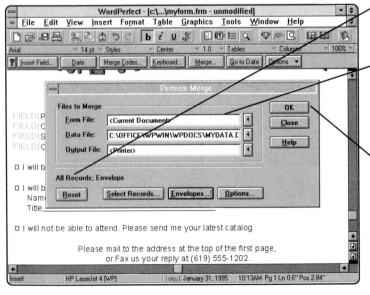

Notice that All Records and Envelopes will be merged.

1. **Confirm** that the Form File and Data File are correct and that <Printer> is in the Output File box.

2. **Click** on **OK**. A "Please wait" message will appear briefly on your screen, then the message you see in the next example will appear.

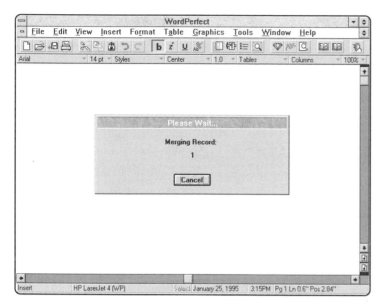

This message box will tell you which records are being merged (sent) to the printer. All the letters will print, then all the envelopes will print. When the letters and envelopes are printed, all dialog boxes will close, and the coded letter will be on your screen again with the cursor at the end of the letter.

PRINTING SELECTED LETTERS FROM A MAILING LIST

The following section will show you how to print selected letters and envelopes rather than the entire mailing list.

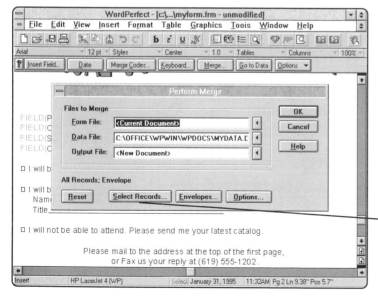

1. **Open** the **coded letter** if it is not already on your screen.

2. **Repeat** the steps to open the Perform Merge dialog box you see here, and select the form file and the data file as you did in the earlier sections.

3. **Click** on **Select Records**. The Select Records dialog box will appear.

4. **Click** on **Record Number Range** to put an ✕ in the box.

5. **Click twice** in the **From box** to highlight the number.

6. **Type** the **number** of the first name for which you want to print a letter. In this example it is name #2.

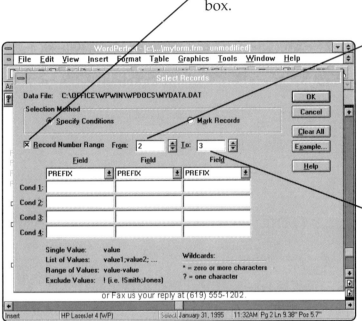

7. **Repeat steps 5 and 6** to type the number of the last name for which you want to print a letter.

8. **Click** on **OK**. The Select Records dialog box will close, and you'll be back at the Perform Merge dialog box.

9. **Click** on the **arrow** to the **right** of the Output File box. A pull-down list will appear.

10. **Click** on **Printer**.

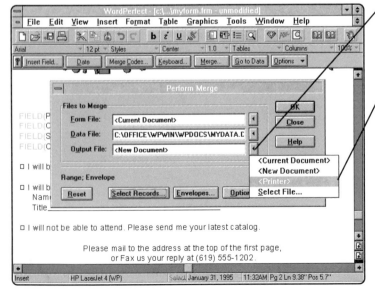

11. **Click** on **OK**. Letters and envelopes for the second and third names in your list will print.

MARKING SPECIFIC LETTERS TO BE PRINTED

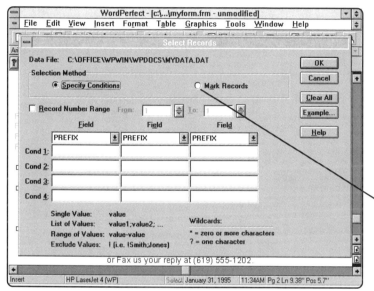

In this section, you'll print letters and envelopes for specifically marked names.

1. **Open** the **coded letter**.

2. **Repeat** the **steps** to open the Select Records dialog box you see here.

3. **Click** on **Mark Records** to put a dot in the circle. After you click, the dialog box will change to look like the one shown below.

Rearranging the Record List

In this example, you'll rearrange the names to show the last name first. This will make it easier to sort through the list.

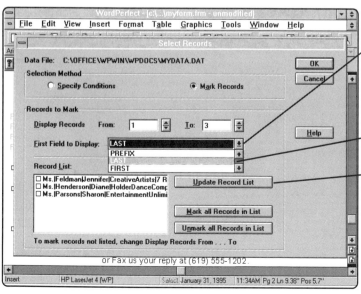

1. **Click** on the ↓ to the **right** of First Field to Display. A pull-down list of field names will appear.

2. **Click** on **LAST**.

3. **Click** on **Update Record List**. The names will be shown with the last name first, as shown in the next example.

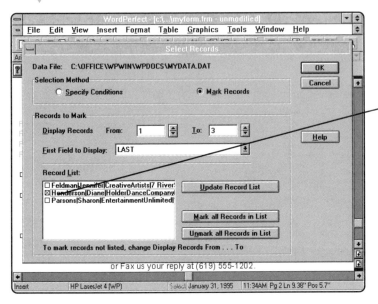

Marking Names

In this example, you'll mark one name in the record list.

1. **Click** on the **second name** in the list to put an ✕ in the box.

2. **Click** on **OK**. The Select Records dialog box will close, and you'll be back at the Perform Merge dialog box.

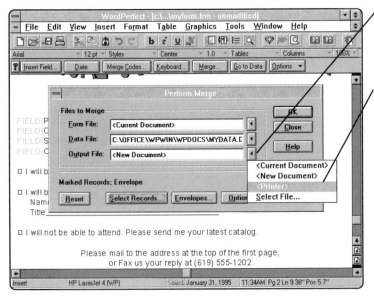

3. **Click** on the **arrow** to the **right** of the Output File box. A pull-down list will appear.

4. **Click** on **<Printer>**.

5. **Click** on **OK** to print letters and envelopes for the marked names.

REMOVING ENVELOPES FROM
THE MERGE PROCESS

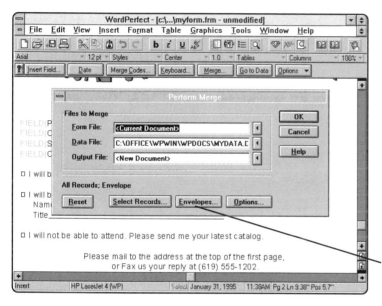

In this section, you'll remove the envelope form that is attached to the letters. Then, you can print letters without printing the attached envelopes.

1. **Repeat steps 1 through 3** at the beginning of the chapter to open the Perform Merge dialog box you see here.

2. **Click** on **Envelopes**. The Envelope Already Exists dialog box will appear.

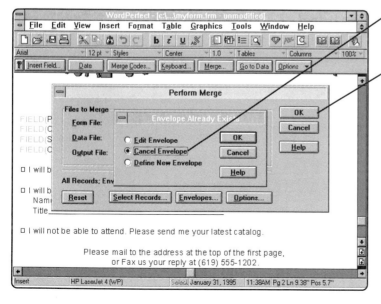

3. **Click** on **Cancel Envelope** to put a dot in the circle.

4. **Click** on **OK**. You'll be returned to the Perform Merge dialog box.

You're now ready to print letters without envelopes.

In the next chapter, you'll print envelopes (without letters) and labels for a mailing list.

Printing Envelopes and Labels for a Mailing List

In Chapter 17, you printed envelopes along with the letters for a mailing list. You can print envelopes separately. You can also print labels for a mailing list. In this chapter, you will do the following:

✔ Merge print envelopes for a mailing list
✔ Merge print labels for a mailing list

OPENING A NEW DOCUMENT

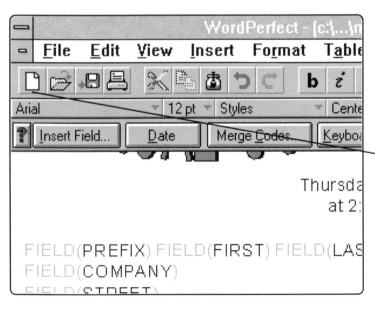

When you want to print only envelopes, you start the process with a new document on your screen. You can open a new document at any time.

1. **Click** on the **New Document button** in the toolbar. A new document will appear on your screen.

CREATING A MERGE ENVELOPE

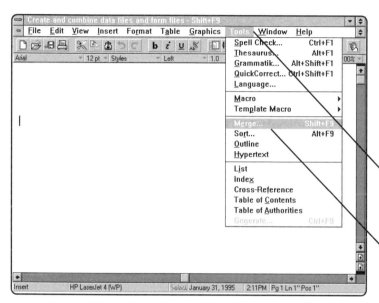

Once you have a new document on your screen, creating a merge envelope is much like the process you followed in Chapter 17 to create the envelope you merged with the letter.

1. **Click** on **Tools** in the menu bar. A pull-down menu will appear.

2. **Click** on **Merge**. The Merge dialog box will appear.

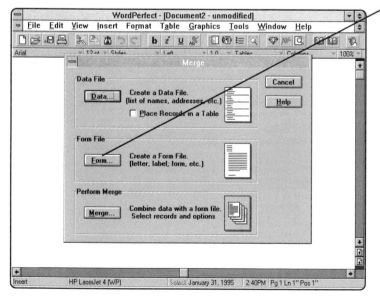

3. **Click** on **Form**. The Create Form File dialog box will appear.

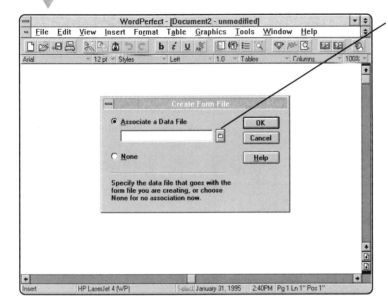

4. **Click** on the **button** to the **right** of the Associate a Data File box. The Select File dialog box will appear.

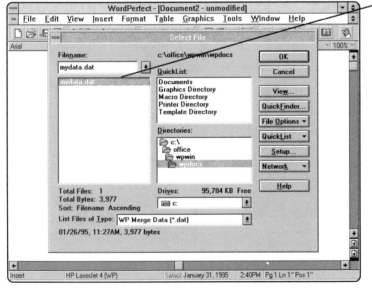

5. **Click twice** on the **name** of the data file. In this example, it is mydata.dat. (You can also click once, then click on OK.)

6. **Click** on **OK** when the Create Form File dialog box reappears (not shown here.) You'll be returned to the new document screen.

Notice that the Merge toolbar has appeared in the document.

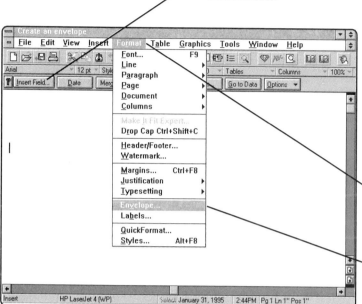

Coding a Merged Envelope

In this section, you'll code an envelope form with the field names from your mailing list.

1. **Click** on **Format** in the menu bar. A pull-down menu will appear.

2. **Click** on **Envelope**. The Envelope dialog box will appear.

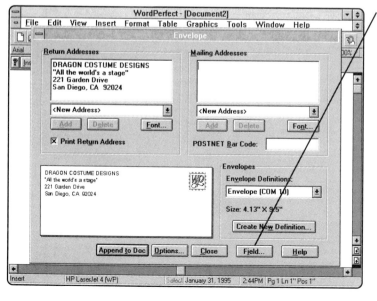

3. **Click** on **Field**. The Insert Field Name or Number dialog box will appear.

4. **Repeat** the appropriate **steps** in the sections entitled, "Printing Envelopes for a Mailing List" and "Adding a USPS Bar Code to the Envelope" on pages 178 through 181 to code the envelope.

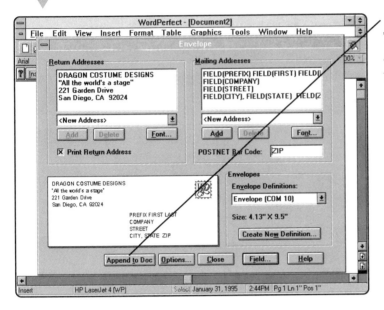

5. Click on **Append to Doc**. The dialog box will close, and a coded envelope form will be on your screen.

MERGE PRINTING ENVELOPES WITHOUT LETTERS

You're now ready to merge print envelopes.

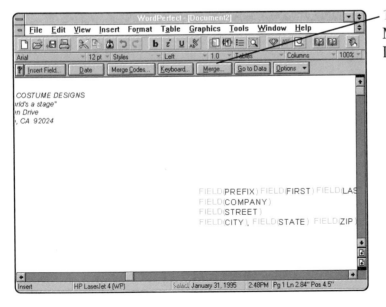

1. Click on **Merge** in the Merge toolbar. The Merge Dialog box will appear.

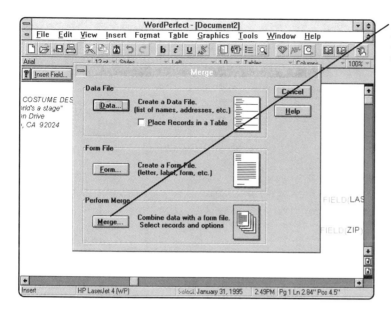

2. **Click** on **Merge**. The Perform Merge dialog box will appear.

3. **Confirm** that <Current Document> is in the Form File box.

4. **Confirm** that the correct data file is in the Data File box.

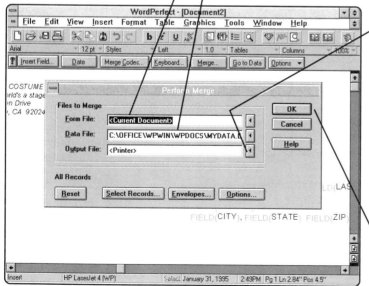

5. **Click** on the **button** to the **right** of the Output File box, and **click** on <**Printer**> in the resulting pull-down list.

Note: You can select specific envelopes to print by following the steps on pages 183 through 186 of Chapter 17.

6. **Click** on **OK**. The envelopes will print.

SAVING THE MERGE
ENVELOPE TEMPLATE

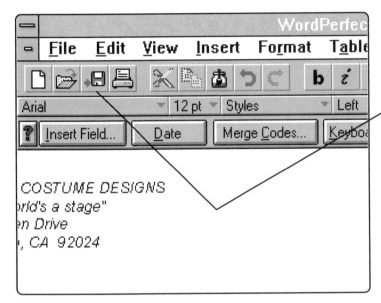

If you routinely print envelopes for a mailing list, you can save the envelope template you just created.

1. **Click** on the **Save button** in the toolbar. The Save As dialog box will appear.

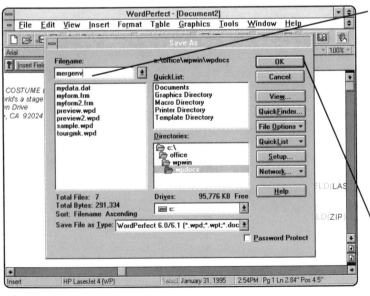

2. **Type** the **name** you want to give the envelope template. It will replace the highlighted *.* that is in the Filename box when this dialog box opens. In this example, the name is mergenv. The name should have no more than eight characters.

3. **Click** on **OK**.

CREATING A MERGE FILE FOR LABELS

In this first section, you'll create a merge file.

1. **Click** on the **New Document button** to open a new document.

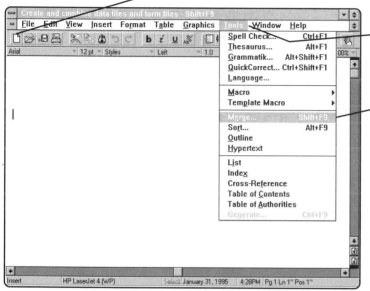

2. **Click** on **Tools** in the menu bar. A pull-down menu will appear.

3. **Click** on **Merge**. The Merge dialog box will appear.

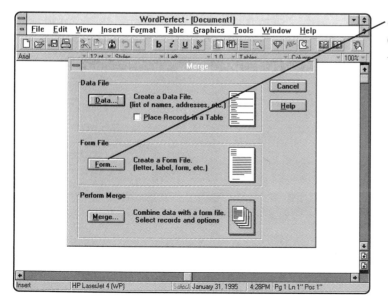

4. **Click** on **Form**. The Create Form File dialog box will appear.

Selecting the Data File

In this section, you'll select the mailing list (data file) for the labels.

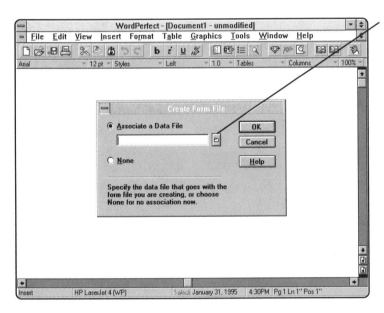

1. **Click** on the **button** to the **right** of the Associate a Data File box. The Select File dialog box will appear.

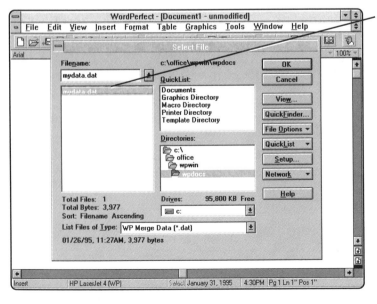

2. **Click twice** on **mydata.dat**. The dialog box will close, and you'll be back at the Create Form File dialog box.

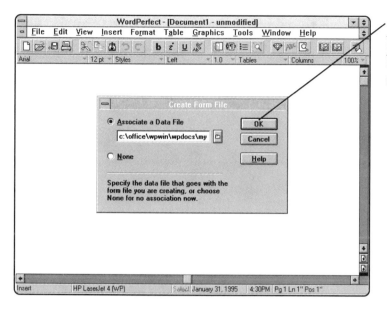

3. **Click** on **OK**. The dialog box will close, and you'll be back at the new document screen.

SETTING UP THE LABEL

In this section, you'll select the appropriate label type.

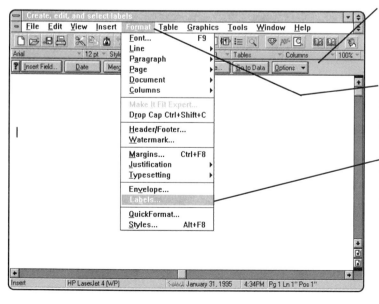

Notice the Merge toolbar has appeared in the document.

1. **Click** on **Format** in the menu bar. A pull-down menu will appear.

2. **Click** on **Labels**. The Labels dialog box will appear.

3. **Click** on the **type** of labels you want to print to put a dot in the circle. In this example, it's Laser labels.

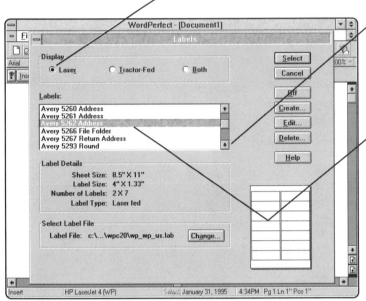

4. **Click** on the ⬇ to scroll through the list of labels. (Check the box of labels for the brand name and number.)

5. **Click** on the **labels** you want to print. In this example, it is Avery 5262. The label display in the lower right corner of the dialog box will change to look like the label setup you chose.

6. **Click** on **Select**. A label format will appear in the document window.

Inserting Field Codes in a Label

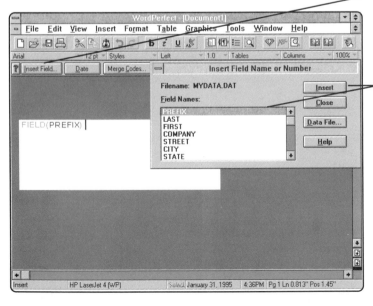

1. **Click** on **Insert Field**. The Insert Field Name or Number dialog box you see here will appear.

2. **Click** on **PREFIX**, then **click** on **Insert**. The PREFIX field will appear in the label.

3. **Repeat step 2** to insert the appropriate fields into the label.

4. When the fields are inserted into the label, **click** on **Close**.

MERGE PRINTING THE LABELS

You're finally ready to print the labels.

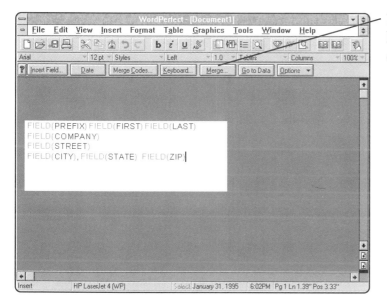

1. Click on **Merge** in the Merge toolbar. The Merge dialog box will appear.

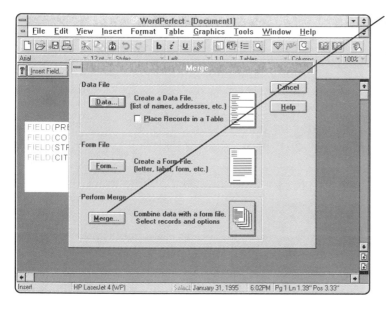

2. Click on **Merge**. The Perform Merge dialog box will appear.

3. **Confirm** that **<Current Document>** is in the Form File box.

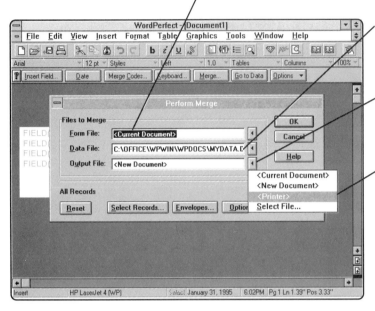

4. **Confirm** that the correct data file is in the Data File box.

5. **Click** on the **arrow** to the **right** of Output File. A pull-down list will appear.

6. **Click** on **<Printer>**.

7. **Click** on **OK**. The labels will be printed. When they are printed, you'll be returned to the label form.

CLOSING THE LABEL FILE

If you print labels for this mailing list frequently, you can save this file. In this example, you'll close the file without saving.

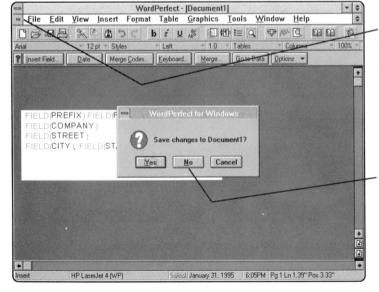

1. **Click twice** on the **Control menu box** (⊟) on the left of the menu bar. A message box will appear asking if you want to save the changes to this document.

2. **Click** on **No** to close the document without saving.

If you click on Yes, the Save As dialog box will appear.

PART IV: INTRODUCING TABLES

CHAPTER

Creating a Table and Using Table Expert

The Tables feature in WordPerfect 6.1 makes it easy to organize information into columns and rows. Once the table is created, it operates like a basic spreadsheet. For example, you can join cells in the table to make room for a heading and increase the numbers of lines in a cell for a large entry. You can choose from a number of predesigned formats in the Table Expert to make your table look professionally designed. In this chapter, you will do the following:

✔ Create a table
✔ Select and apply a formatting style from Table Expert
✔ Join cells
✔ Enter text and numbers

CREATING A TABLE

In this example you will create a table that has four columns and six rows. Although you can insert a table anywhere in an existing document, in this example you will open a new document for the table if you do not already have a blank document on your screen.

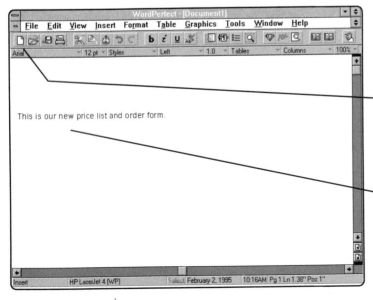

1. **Click** on the **New Document button** in the toolbar. A blank document will appear on your screen.

2. **Type** the sentence **This is our new price list and order form**, then **press Enter twice**.

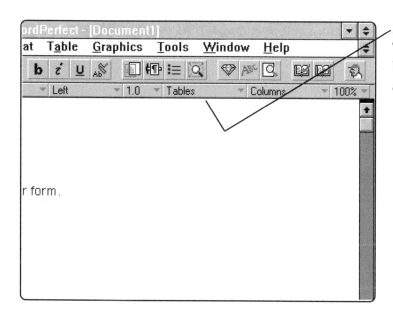

3. **Press and hold** on the **Tables button** on the Power Bar. A pull-down grid will appear.

4. **Press and hold** the **mouse button** and **drag** your **pointer** until you have highlighted **4 columns and 6 rows**. (The heading at the top of the grid will show 4×6.)

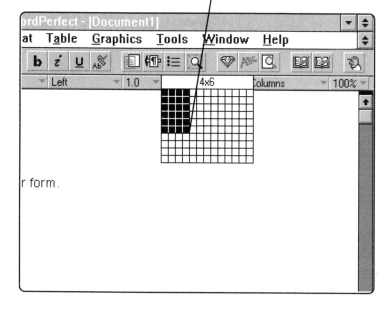

5. **Release** the **mouse button**. The grid will disappear, and a table will appear in your document.

You can also create a table by clicking on Table in the menu bar then clicking on Create in the pull-down menu. But it's not nearly as much fun as using the Table button.

USING TABLE EXPERT

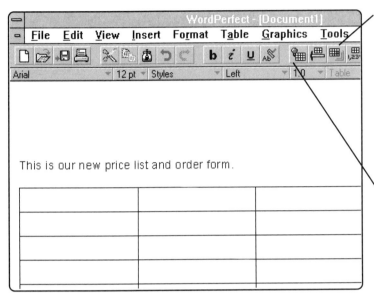

Notice that a specialized toolbar appeared automatically when you created a table.

1. **Click** in the **first cell** of the table if the cursor isn't there already.

2. **Click** on the **Table Expert button** in the toolbar. The Table Expert dialog box will appear.

3. **Click** on the **first style** in the Available Styles list. A formatted table in that style will appear to the right.

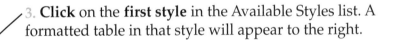

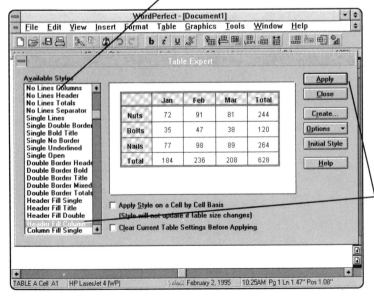

4. **Click** on several styles on the list and notice the changes in the sample to the right. If you have a color printer, you can create some very exciting table formats, but there are terrific designs for a regular black and white printer as well.

5. When the highlight bar is on **Header Fill Column**, **click** on **Apply**.

JOINING CELLS

When you join cells you remove the dividing lines between them to create a single, larger cell. In this section you will join the cells in the first row to create a single cell for a heading.

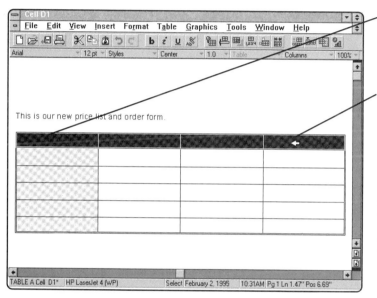

1. **Click** in cell **A1** to place the cursor if it is not already there.

2. **Press and hold** the **mouse button** and **drag** the highlight bar **across** the first row of the table to D1.

You'll notice that the mouse pointer changes shape with annoying frequency when you work with tables.

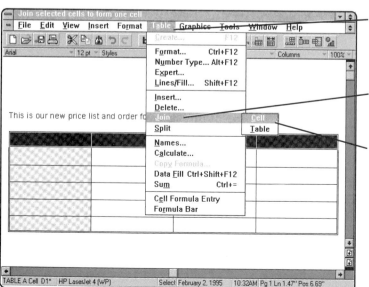

3. **Click** on **Table** in the menu bar. A pull-down menu will appear.

4. **Click** on **Join**. Another menu will appear.

5. **Click** on **Cell**. The dividing lines will be removed from the highlighted cells.

ENTERING TEXT
AND NUMBERS IN A TABLE

You enter and edit text in a table just as you would in the document itself.

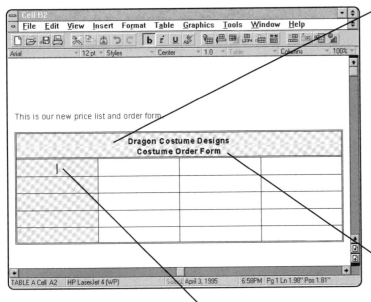

1. **Click** on the **first row** in the table if your cursor is not already there.

2. **Type Dragon Costume Designs**. Notice that the table format you applied centers the text automatically.

3. **Press Enter**. This will add a line to the cell you are in.

4. **Type Costume Order Form**.

5. **Press** the **Tab key** on your keyboard. This will move you to the next cell, which is in the first column.

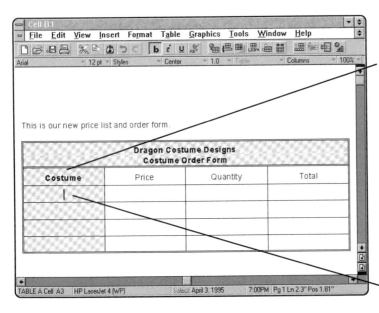

6. **Type** the following words, **pressing** the **Tab key** after each word.

Costume
Price
Quantity
Total.

Notice that each word is centered automatically.

7. **Press** the **Tab key** to move to the next cell.

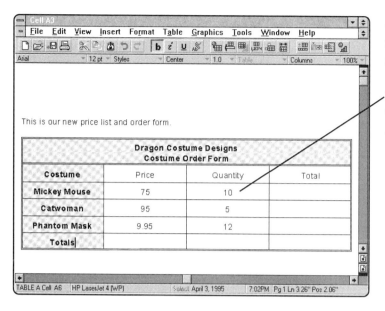

8. Type the words and numbers you see in this example.

When you type 10, press the Tab key twice to move to the first column.

SAVING THE TABLE

1. **Click** on the **Save button** in the toolbar. It's the third button from the left. The Save As dialog box will appear.

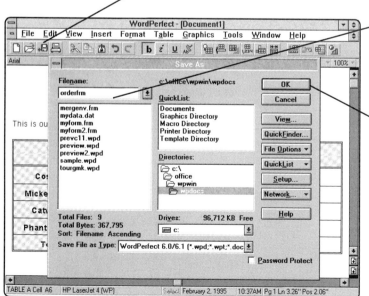

2. Type orderfrm. It will replace the highlighted *.*. A filename should have no more than eight characters.

3. **Click** on **OK**. The dialog box will close.

Editing a Table

You can sort data in a table (or in a list) alphabetically and numerically. You can add and delete rows and columns with ease. You can change the position of a table on the printed page. You can also remove the grid lines from the table. In this chapter, you will do the following:

✔ Sort data alphabetically and numerically
✔ Add and delete a row to a table
✔ Change column width
✔ Change the position of a table so that it is centered across the page
✔ Remove the grid lines from a table

SORTING DATA ALPHABETICALLY

You can sort data in a document and in a table. In this example you will sort the data in rows 3 through 5 alphabetically by the first cell in each row. Because you do not want to sort the entire table, you will highlight the rows you want to sort.

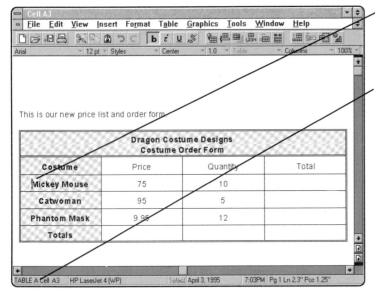

1. **Click** to the **left** of **Mickey Mouse** to place the cursor.

Notice that the status bar at the bottom of the screen tells you that this is Table A Cell A3. It's "Table A" because it's the first table in the document. Columns in a table are labeled A through, in this case, D and rows are given numbers. Therefore, it's "Cell A3" because it's in column A, the third row.

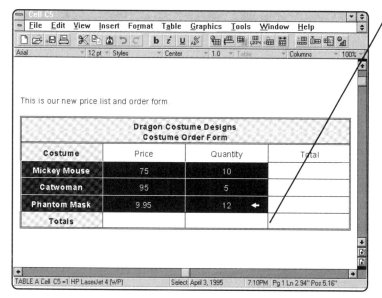

2. **Press and hold** the **mouse button** and **drag** the highlight bar down to **C5**. Notice that the mouse pointer changes shape as you drag. (Because there are no numbers in column D, the "Total" column, you don't have to highlight the cells in column D.)

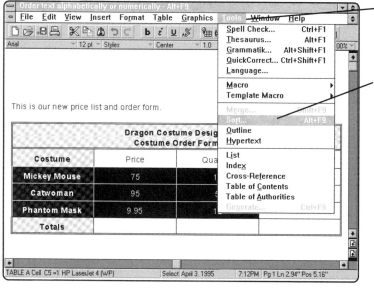

3. **Click** on **Tools** in the menu bar. A pull-down menu will appear.

4. **Click** on **Sort**. The Sort dialog box will appear.

WordPerfect 6.1 has a number of predefined sorts and, fortunately, it has a sort based on the first cell in a table row, which is exactly what you want for this example.

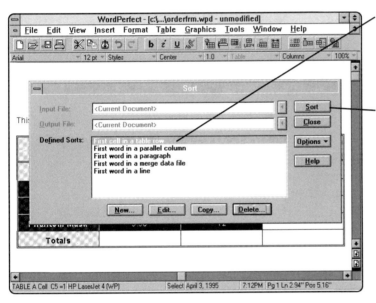

Notice that First cell in a table row is highlighted when you open this dialog box.

5. **Click** on **Sort**. The dialog box will close, and the data will be sorted alphabetically based on the first cell in each row.

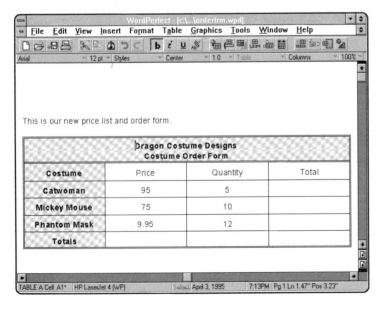

Your screen will look like this example. Pretty neat, don't you think?

SORTING DATA NUMERICALLY

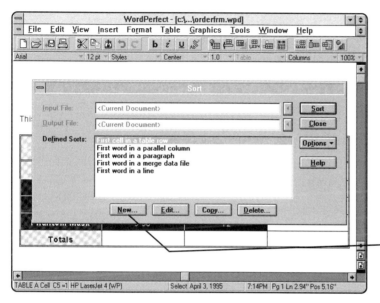

In this next section, you'll sort the data in this table by the price of each item, putting the least expensive item first.

1. **Repeat steps 1 through 4** in the previous section to highlight the same cells and open the Sort dialog box you see here.

2. **Click** on **New**. The New Sort dialog box will appear.

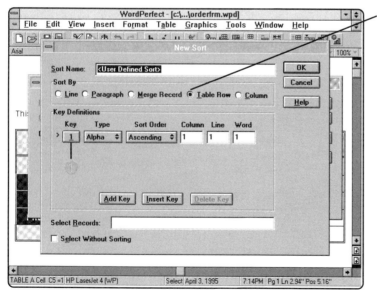

Table Row is already selected because WordPerfect knows what you highlighted.

The Key Definitions tell WordPerfect how to sort lines:

❶ **Key = 1** means that you will sort on one criterion. You can sort on up to nine criteria. Consult *WordPerfect 6.1 Reference Manual* for directions on more complicated sorting procedures.

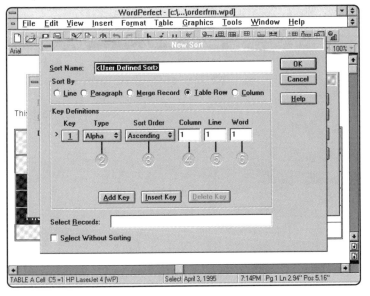

❷ **Type = Alpha** means it is set for an alphabetic sort.

❸ **Sort Order = Ascending** means the sort is in ascending order (from A to Z or 1 to N).

❹ **Column = 1** means WordPerfect will sort the lines based on the first column.

❺ **Line = 1** means the sort will be made on the first line in the cell. For example, only the company name in the first cell would be used in the sort (if that cell were highlighted).

❻ **Word = 1** means WordPerfect will sort on the first word in the cell. For example, in Phantom Mask the sort will be on "Phantom" rather than on "Mask."

Defining a Numeric Sort

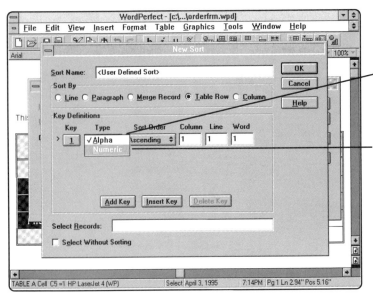

1. **Click and hold** on the **Type box**. A pull-down list will appear.

2. **Continue to hold** the **mouse button,** and **drag** the highlight bar down to **Numeric** then **release** the **mouse button**. "Numeric" will appear in the Type box.

3. **Confirm** that **Ascending** is in the Sort Order box.

4. **Click twice** in the **Column box** to highlight the number 1 that is there.

5. **Type 2** to tell WordPerfect to sort on the prices in the second column.

6. **Click** on **OK**. The Sort dialog box will reappear.

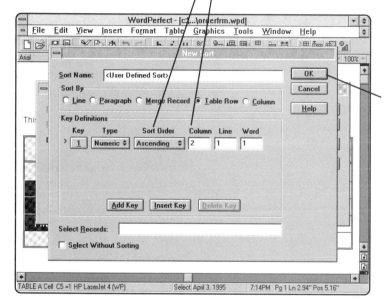

Notice the <User Defined Sort> option that is now in the Defined Sorts list. This is the sort you just defined. This sort will stay on the list, and you can select it at any time.

7. **Click** on **Sort**. The dialog box will close, and the table will appear with the data sorted by the second column.

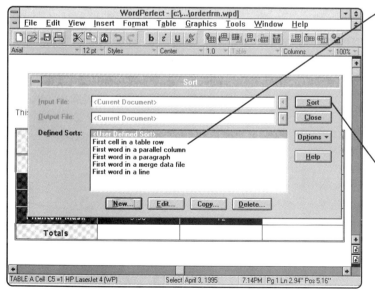

ADDING A ROW (OR COLUMN)

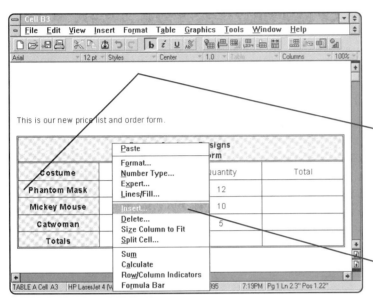

You can add a row (or column) anywhere in the table. In this example you will add a row after row 3 using a quick menu.

1. **Click** on **Phantom Mask** in row 3 to place the cursor.

2. **Click** the **right mouse button**. A quick menu will appear.

3. **Click** on **Insert**. The Insert Columns/Rows dialog box will appear.

4. **Click** on **Rows** if it does not already have a dot in the circle. (You would click on Columns if you wanted to add a column to the table.)

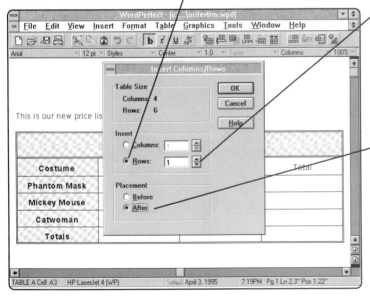

Notice that you can add as many rows as you want by clicking on the ▲ to the right of the rows box. In this example you will add 1 row.

5. **Click** on **After** to insert a dot in the circle.

6. **Click** on **OK**. A row will be added to the table after row 3.

DELETING A ROW (OR COLUMN)

You can delete a row or column as easily as you added one. In this example you will delete the row you just added.

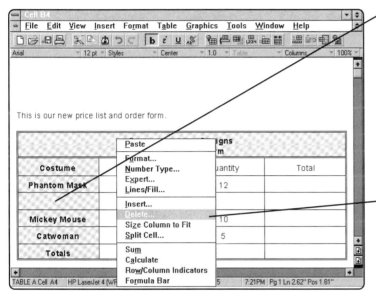

1. **Click** in the row you want to delete. In this example, **click** in the **new row** if your cursor is not already there.

2. **Press** the **right mouse button** to bring up the quick menu.

3. **Click** on **Delete**. The Delete dialog box will appear.

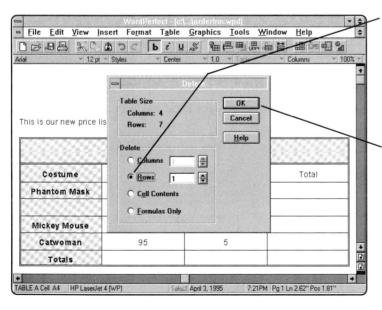

4. **Click** on **Rows** if it does not already have a dot in the circle. (You would click on Columns if you wanted to delete the column where the cursor is placed.)

5. **Click** on **OK**. The row will be deleted.

CHANGING COLUMN WIDTH

You'll be pleasantly surprised at the ease with which you can change column width.

1. **Click anywhere** in the second column to place the cursor.

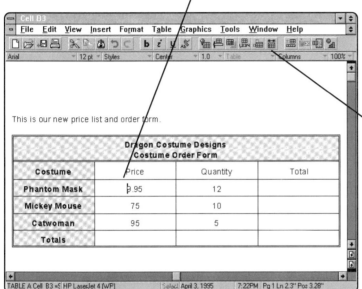

2. **Click** on the **Size Column to Fit button** in the toolbar. It's the fifth from the right. The columns will be sized to fit the longest entry.

3. **Repeat steps 1 and 2** to automatically size the third column.

CHANGING FONT SIZE

In this example, you'll increase the size of the font in the company name.

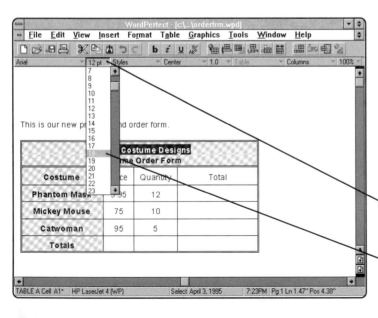

1. **Click** to the **left** of **Dragon** then **press and hold** the **mouse button** and **drag** the highlight bar over the company name.

2. **Click** on the **Font Size button** in the Power Bar.

3. **Click** on **18** to increase the font size to 18 points.

CHANGING TEXT ALIGNMENT

You can change the alignment that is set up by the Table Expert formatting.

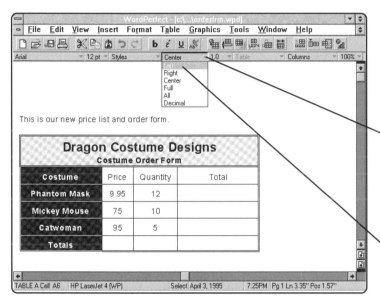

1. **Click** to the **left** of **Costume** in cell A2, then **press and hold** the **mouse button** and **drag** the cursor down the column to Totals in A6.

2. **Click** on the **Alignment button** in the Power Bar. (The button currently reads Center to show that the text is centered.)

3. **Click** on **Left**. The text in the highlighted cells will be left-aligned.

CENTERING A TABLE

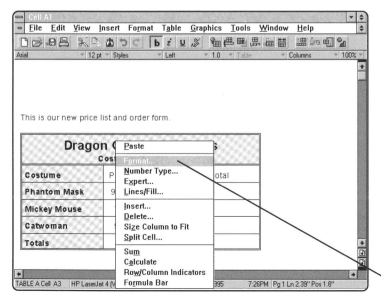

When you create a table, it goes across the entire page. When you change column width, the right edge of the table moves. You can center the table easily.

1. **Click anywhere** in the table to place the cursor.

2. **Click** the **right mouse button** to open a quick menu.

3. **Click** on **Format**.

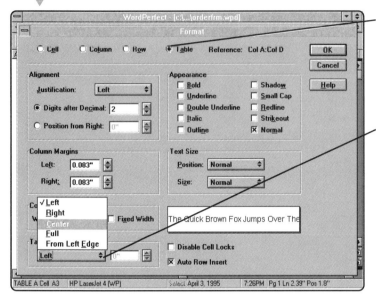

4. **Click** on **Table** to insert a dot in the circle. The dialog box will change to show options associated with a table.

5. **Click and hold** on **Left** in the Table Position box. A pop-up list will appear.

6. **Continue to hold** the **mouse button** and **drag** the highlight bar to **Center**, then **release** the **mouse button**.

7. **Click** on **OK**. The dialog box will close, and your table will be centered across the page.

REMOVING GRID LINES

You can remove the grid lines from a table. They will be removed from the screen and from the printed page.

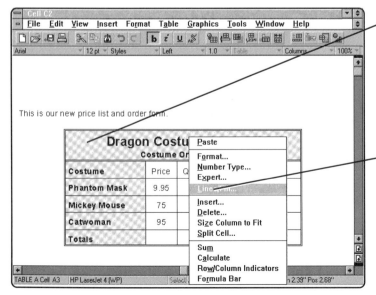

1. **Click anywhere** in the table to place the cursor.

2. **Click** the **right mouse button**. A quick menu will appear.

3. **Click** on **Lines/Fill**. The Lines/Fill dialog box will appear.

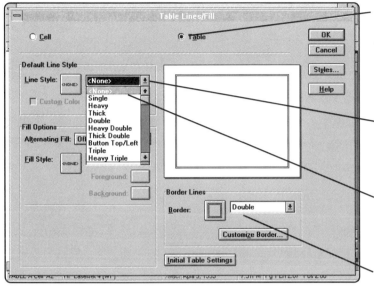

4. **Click** on **Table** to insert a dot in the circle. The dialog box will change to show options appropriate for tables.

5. **Click** on the ⬇ to the right of Line Style. A pull-down list will appear.

6. **Click** on **<None>**. The internal grid lines will be removed.

Notice that you can also change the border lines that surround the table. In this example, you won't change the border lines.

7. **Click** on **OK** to close the dialog box. The table will appear with no internal grid lines.

8. **Click** on the **Undo button** in the toolbar to put the lines back in the table.

9. **Click** on the **Save button** on the toolbar to save your work.

CHAPTER

21

Writing Formulas and Formatting Numbers

You can format numbers to have decimal places, commas, and dollar signs. You can also write formulas in tables that will perform mathematical functions. In this chapter, you will do the following:

✔ Write formulas for multiplication and addition
✔ Copy a formula to other cells
✔ Change the format of numbers
✔ Change the alignment of numbers
✔ Delete a table from a document

OPENING THE FORMULA BAR

When you have a table on your screen, you can open a special formula bar at the click of your mouse.

1. **Click anywhere** in the table to place the cursor.

2. **Click** on the **Formula Bar button**. It's the fourth from the right in the toolbar. The formula bar you see here will appear.

WRITING FORMULAS

You can write formulas in your table that will perform mathematical functions. The most common functions and their symbols are as follows:

Function	Symbol	Example
Addition	+	D3+D4+D5
Subtraction	-	B4-C4
Multiplication	*	B3*C3
Division	/	B2/B3

Writing a Multiplication Formula

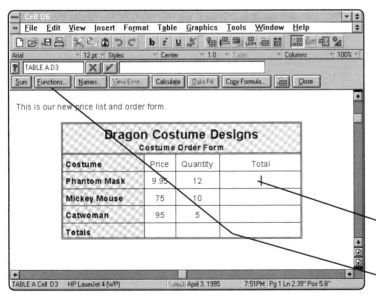

In this example you will write a formula to calculate the total in column D by multiplying the price in column B times the quantity in column C. You will write the formula for row 3, then later in the chapter you will copy the formula to rows 4 and 5.

1. **Click** on **D3** to place the cursor.

2. **Click** on the **Functions button** in the Formula bar. The Table Functions dialog box will appear.

3. **Press and hold** on the **scroll button** and **drag** it **down** the scroll bar until you see PRODUCT (List).

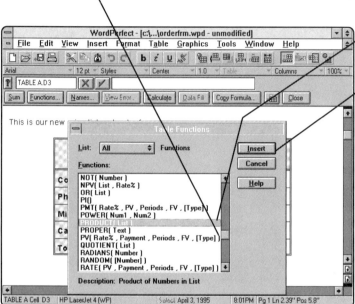

4. **Click** on PRODUCT (List) to highlight it.

5. **Click** on **Insert**. The Table Functions dialog box will close.

6. **Type b3*c3**. It will replace the highlighted text in the Formula bar.

7. **Click** on ✔ to the left of your formula. The results of the formula (119.4) will be entered into cell D3.

Copying a Formula

In this section you will copy the formula in D3 to D4 and D5.

1. **Click** in **D3**, which is the cell whose formula you want to copy. If you've been following along with this chapter, your cursor is already in D3.

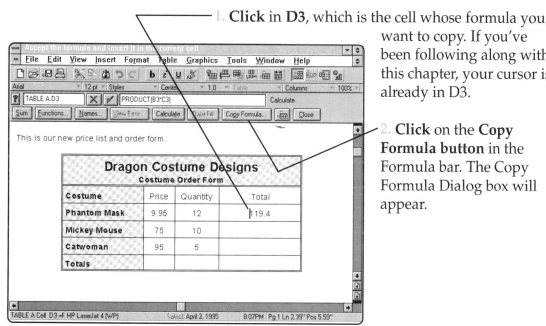

2. **Click** on the **Copy Formula button** in the Formula bar. The Copy Formula Dialog box will appear.

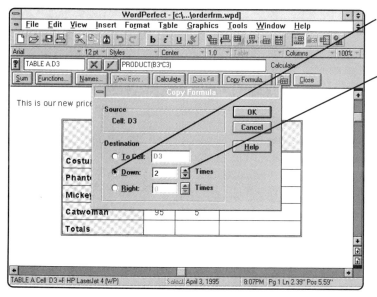

3. **Click** on **Down** to put a dot in the circle.

4. **Click once** on the ▲ to make the number in the Down box 2. This means the formula will be copied down to the next two cells.

5. **Click** on **OK**. The Copy Formula dialog box will close, and the formula will be copied to D4 and D5.

USING THE SUM FUNCTION

WordPerfect has a special button that sums the cells above the cell with the cursor.

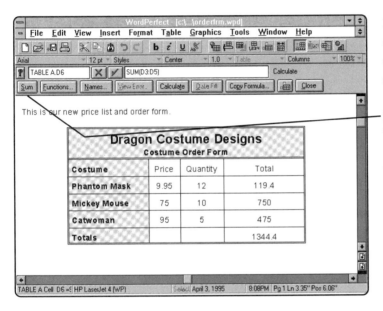

1. **Click** in cell **D6** (the last cell in the table) to place the cursor. On your screen, the cell will be empty.

2. **Click** on the **Sum button**. The sum of D3 through D5 (1344.4) will be inserted into D6.

CHANGING THE NUMBER TYPE

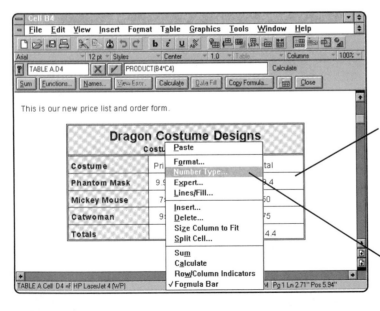

In this section, you'll change the numbers in column D to a currency format (two decimal places and a dollar sign).

1. **Click anywhere** in column D to place the cursor.

2. **Click** the **right mouse button**. A quick menu will appear.

3. **Click** on **Number Type**. The Number Type dialog box will appear.

4. **Click** on **Column** to put a dot in the circle. This will format the entire column.

5. **Click** on **Currency** to put a dot in the circle. Notice that the Preview box at the bottom of the dialog box shows an example of a number in the Currency format.

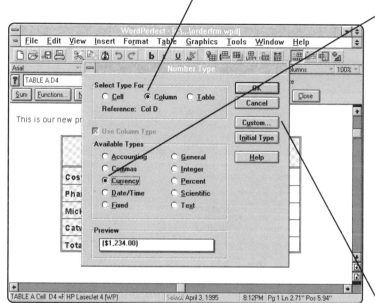

Customizing the Number Type

In this example, you'll remove the dollar sign from the currency format.

1. **Click** on **Custom**. The Customize Number Type dialog box will appear.

2. **Click** on **Use Currency Symbol** to *remove* the ✕ from the box.

3. **Click** on **OK** to close the Customize Number Type dialog box. You'll return to the Number Type dialog box.

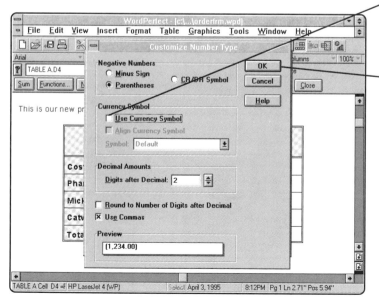

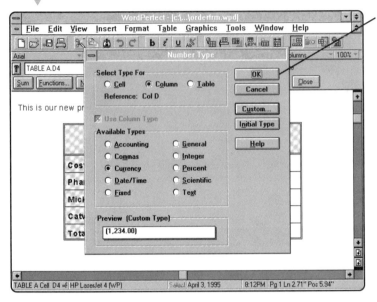

4. **Click** on **OK** to close the Number Type dialog box.

CHANGING NUMBER ALIGNMENT

In this section, you'll format the numbers in column D to align at the decimal point. Because you don't want to change the alignment of the column heading, you'll highlight the cells whose alignment you want to change.

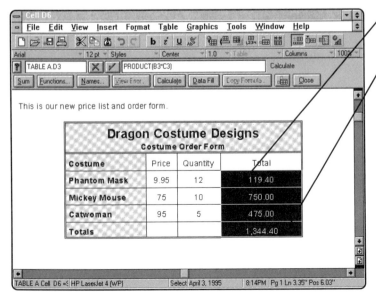

1. **Click** to the **left of 119.40** to place the cursor.

2. **Press and hold** the **mouse button** and **drag** the **cursor** down to 1,344.40 in the last cell to highlight cells D3 through D6 as you see here.

3. **Click** on the **Justification button** in the Power Bar. A pull-down list of alignments will appear.

4. **Click** on **Decimal**. The numbers in column D will be aligned at the decimal point.

5. **Click anywhere** to remove the highlighting.

6. **Click** on the **Save button** in the toolbar to save your work. It's the third button from the left.

DELETING A TABLE

To delete the table, you must highlight it first.

1. **Place** the **mouse pointer** in the first cell of the table just under the top line. The mouse pointer should be in the shape you see here. You'll probably have to fiddle quite a bit with the placement of the pointer to get it to change to this shape.

2. **Press and hold** the **mouse button** and **drag** the **mouse pointer** down the table. The pointer will change shape to a left-pointing arrow as you drag. The entire table will be highlighted.

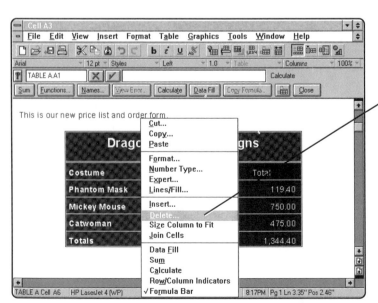

3. **Click** the **right mouse button** to bring up a quick menu.

4. **Click** on **Delete**. The Delete Table dialog box will appear.

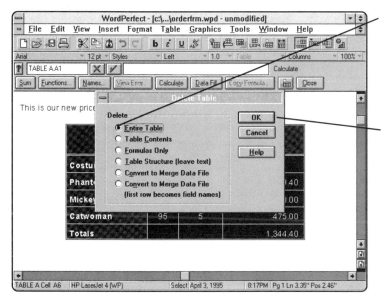

Notice that Entire Table is already selected (has a dot in the circle) because WordPerfect knows you highlighted the entire table.

5. **Click** on **OK**. The entire table will be deleted.

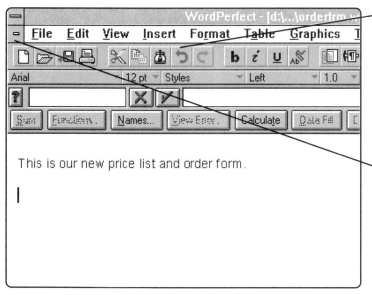

6. **Click** on the **Undo button** to get the table back. This will work, of course, only if you haven't performed any other function between the delete and the Undo.

7. **Click twice** on the **Control menu box** (▭) to the left of the menu bar. You'll be asked if you want to save changes. Click on the appropriate answer.

PART V: WORKING SMARTER

CHAPTER

Creating a Directory and Moving Files

WordPerfect has terrific file management capabilities. You can create directories and move and copy files without ever leaving WordPerfect! In this chapter, you will do the following:

✔ Create a new directory
✔ Move files to the newly created directory
✔ Open a file in a new directory

CREATING A NEW DIRECTORY

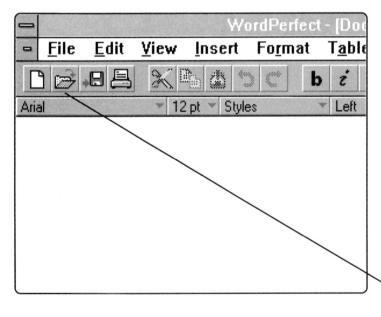

WordPerfect is set up to store files in the "wpdocs" directory, which is a subdirectory of "wpwin." As you create more and more files, you may want to store all files of a certain type in a specific directory. For example, in this chapter you will create a special subdirectory for your mail merge form letters and data files.

1. **Click** on the **Open button** in the toolbar. The Open File dialog box will appear.

Selecting the Location

A file directory is organized like a term paper outline. If a topic is of major importance, it's a main heading (or *directory*, in computer talk). If the subject is part of a broader topic, it's a subheading under the broader topic (or a *subdirectory*, in computer talk). In this example, you're going to create a new subdirectory for your mail merge forms and data files.

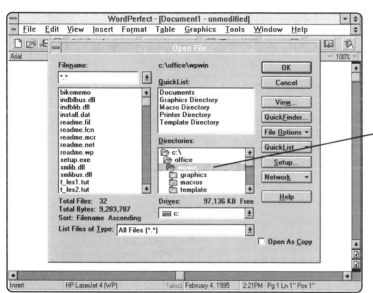

1. **Click twice** on **wpwin**. A list of the subdirectories under this heading will appear as you see here. By clicking on this directory, you will create a new subheading (or subdirectory) under wpwin.

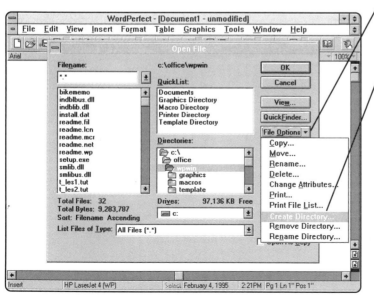

2. **Click** on **File Options**. A drop-down menu will appear.

3. **Click** on **Create Directory**. The Create Directory dialog box will appear.

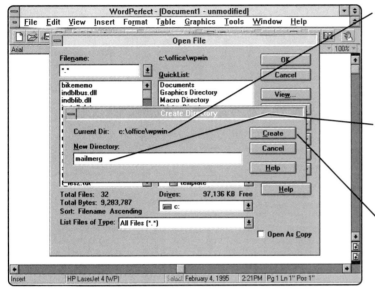

Notice that "c:\office\wpwin" is listed as the current directory. The new directory will go under the wpwin directory.

4. **Type mailmerg**. Like filenames, directory names can have no more than eight characters.

5. **Click** on **Create**. The dialog box will close, and you'll be back at the Open File dialog box.

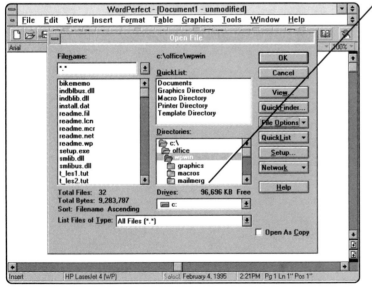

Notice that the "mailmerg" subdirectory is now listed in alphabetical order along with the other subdirectories of wpwin.

MOVING FILES
BETWEEN DIRECTORIES

In this section, you'll move the mail merge form letter and data file to the new directory, which we called "mailmerg." (Although "mailmerg" is technically a subdirectory, the terms subdirectory and directory are used interchangeably.)

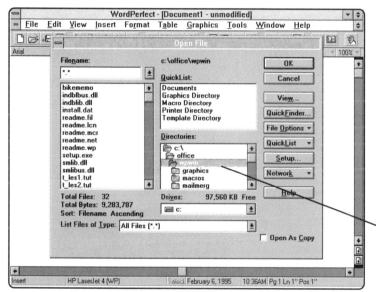

1. **Repeat** the **steps** at the beginning of the chapter to open the Open File dialog box if it isn't already on your screen.

2. **Click twice** on **wpwin** to open a list of all subdirectories under wpwin as you see here.

3. **Click** on the ⬇ to scroll through the list of subdirectories until you can see mailmerg.

4. Because the files you want to move are located in the wpdocs directory, **click twice** on **wpdocs**. The files in that directory will appear in the Filename list on the left side of the dialog box.

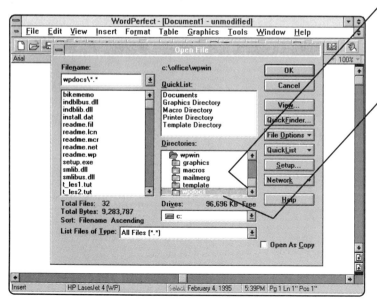

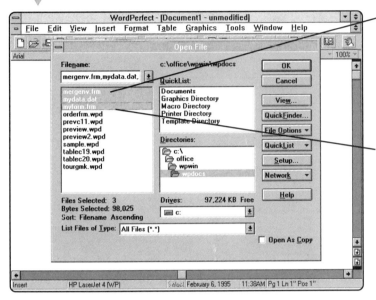

5. **Click** on the **first file** you want to move to highlight it.

6. **Press and hold** the **Shift key** on your keyboard.

7. **Click** on the **last file** you want to move. All files between clicks will be highlighted. (If the files are not in sequence, press and hold the Ctrl key as you click on individual files.)

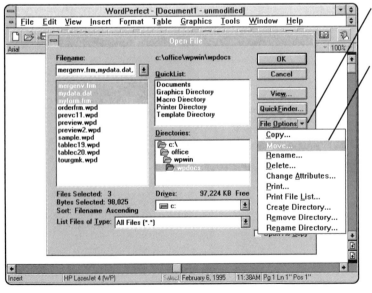

8. **Click** on **File Options**. A pull-down menu will appear.

9. **Click** on **Move**. The Move Files dialog box will appear.

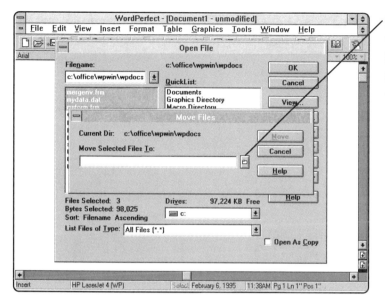

10. **Click** on the **button** to the **right** of the Move Selected Files To box. The Select Directory dialog box will appear.

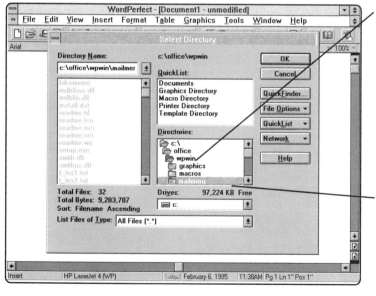

11. **Click twice** on **wpwin**. (If you can't see the directory you want, click twice on c:\ at the top of the list. This will open a list of all the directories on C drive. Then, scroll through the list until you see the directory you want.)

12. **Click** on **mailmerg**.

13. **Click** on **OK**.

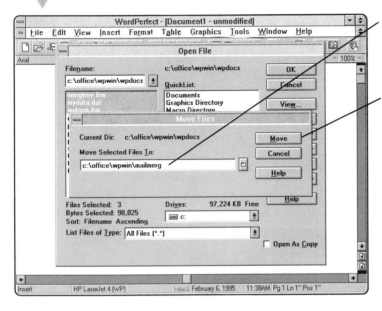

14. **Confirm** that the correct directory is shown in the Move Selected Files To box.

15. **Click** on **Move**. You'll go back to the Open File dialog box.

16. **Click** on **Cancel** to close the Open File dialog box.

OPENING A FILE IN A NEW DIRECTORY

WordPerfect is set up to go directly to the wpdocs directory. In this section, you'll open a file that is in another directory.

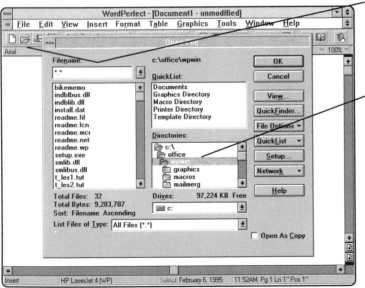

1. **Click** on the **Open button** in the toolbar. The Open File dialog box you see here will appear.

2. **Click twice** on **wpwin**. A list of directories will appear under wpwin. (If you don't see the directory, click twice on c:\ at the top of the list. This will open a list of all directories on C drive. Then, scroll through the list until you see the directory you want.)

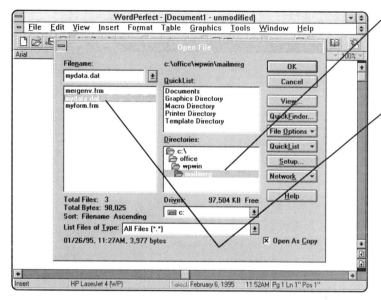

3. **Click twice** on **mailmerg**. A list of files in this directory will appear in the Filename list on the left.

4. **Click twice** on the **name of the file** you want to open. In this example, it is mydata.dat. The file will open on your screen (not shown here).

When you close the file, the filename will be listed on the File pull-down menu. If you want to open it again, you can use the menu instead of going through the Open File dialog box as you did above. Remember, though, that the File pull-down menu lists only the four most recently used files. As you create and use other files, their names will replace the names of files previously used. When the name is no longer listed on the File pull-down menu, simply repeat the steps above to open the file through the Open File dialog box.

Also, the Open File dialog box remembers the directory you opened last. When you next go into the Open File dialog box, you may have to change directories as you did above.

Using QuickCorrect and Abbreviations

Most people have text that they use over and over again, such as a letter closing. WordPerfect has two ways you can store a frequently used item so that you can insert it into your document quickly. The first is Abbreviations, which allows you to insert a word or phrase into your document by typing a few keystrokes. QuickCorrect lets you create an automatic correction for common phrases, such as ASAP, or words that you regularly misspell or type incorrectly. In this chapter, you will do the following:

✓ Setup and use Abbreviations
✓ Setup and use QuickCorrect

USING ABBREVIATIONS

Abbreviations is an excellent program for storing and inserting text that you use regularly, such as the closing to a letter.

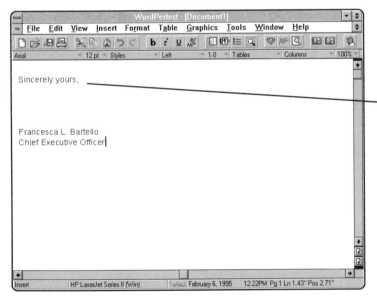

Creating an Abbreviations Entry

1. **Type** a **closing** that you use for your letters. In this example, we used a closing for Francesca L. Bartello, Chief Executive Officer.

2. **Click** to the **left** of the letter "**S**" in Sincerely to set the cursor.

3. **Press and hold** the **mouse button** as you **drag** it **down** to highlight the closing text.

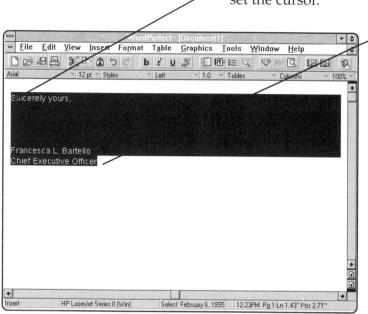

4. **Click** on **Insert** in the menu bar. A pull-down menu will appear.

5. **Click** on **Abbreviations**. The Abbreviations dialog box will appear.

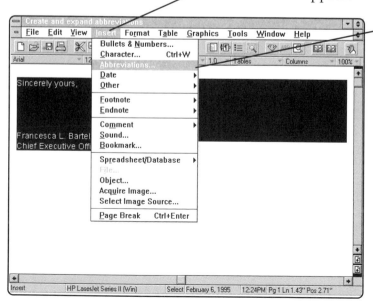

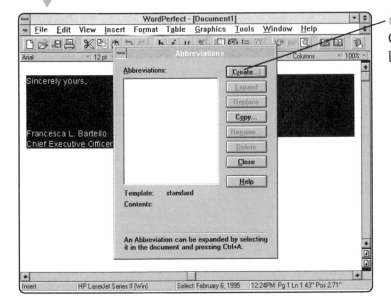

6. **Click** on **Create**. The Create Abbreviation dialog box will open.

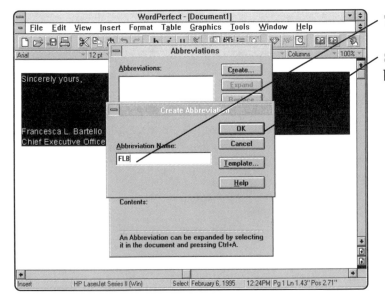

7. **Type FLB**.

8. **Click** on **OK**. The dialog box will close.

Notice that "FLB" shows in the Abbreviations list.

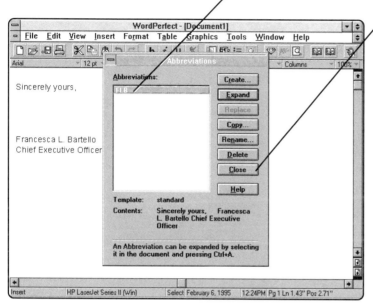

9. **Click** on **Close**. The dialog box will close.

Inserting an Abbreviation

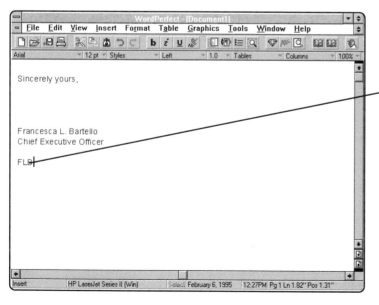

1. **Press** the **Enter key twice** to move the cursor down two lines.

2. **Type FLB**.

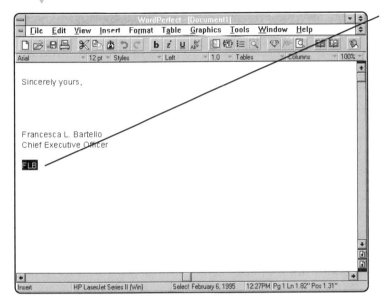

3. **Click twice** to the **left** of **"FLB."** The text will be highlighted.

4. **Press and hold** the **Ctrl key** as you **press** the **letter a** on your keyboard (ctrl + a). The Abbreviation "FLB" will be replaced by the closing you created.

CREATING A QUICKCORRECT ENTRY

In this section, you'll create a QuickCorrect entry that will automatically replace "asap" with "as soon as possible."

1. **Press** the **Enter key twice** to move down two lines.

2. **Type** "**Call me.**"

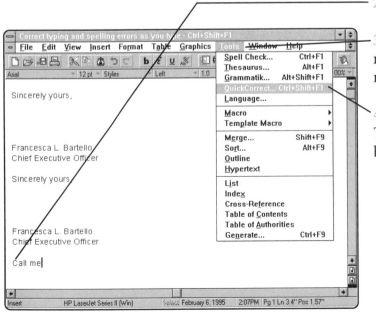

3. **Click** on **Tools** in the menu bar. A pull-down menu will appear.

4. **Click** on **QuickCorrect**. The QuickCorrect dialog box will appear.

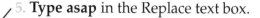

5. **Type asap** in the Replace text box.

6. **Press** the **Tab key**.

7. **Type** "**as soon as possible**" in the With text box.

8. **Click** on **Add Entry**.

9. **Click** on **Replace Words as You Type** to put an X in the box if one is not already there.

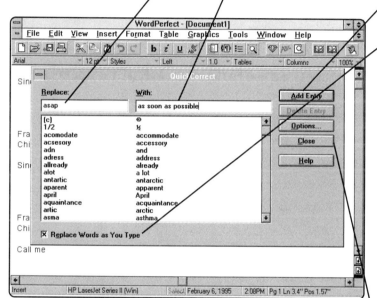

Before you do step 10, scroll through the list to see the number of automatic corrections WordPerfect has already included. If you have your own personal spelling or typing demons, you can add them to this list by repeating steps 5 through 8.

10. **Click** on **Close**.

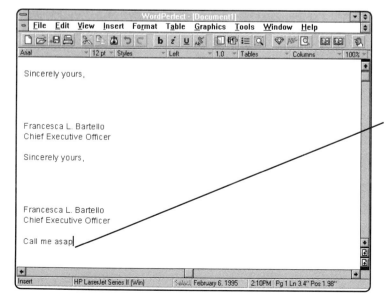

Inserting a QuickCorrect Item

1. **Press** the **Spacebar once** and **type** "**asap**."

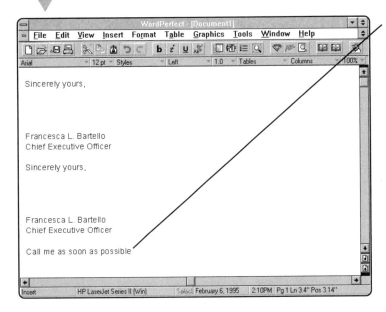

2. **Press** the **Spacebar once**. Zap! "Asap" is replaced by the new text.

CLOSING DOCUMENT1

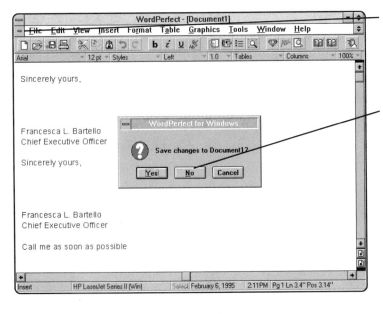

1. **Click twice** on the **Control menu box** (▭) on the menu bar. A WordPerfect dialog box will appear.

2. **Click** on **No**. The document will close without being saved.

Using the Fax Expert

If you have a fax program for Windows installed on your system, you can send faxes directly through WordPerfect 6.1, using the Print dialog box. If you're sending a "traditional" fax through a fax machine, you can create a dynamite looking cover sheet to send with it. This chapter will concentrate on creating a fax cover sheet. In this chapter, you will do the following:

✔ Create a personalized fax cover sheet template
✔ Create an Address Book

OPENING THE FAX EXPERT

1. **Click** on **File** in the menu bar. A pull-down menu will appear.

2. **Click** on **New**. The New Document dialog box will appear.

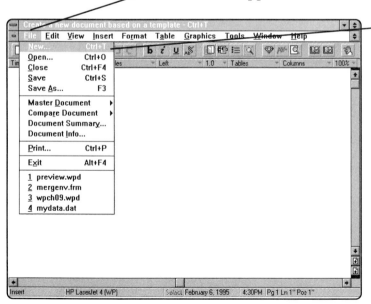

3. **Clic**k on **Fax** in the Group List.

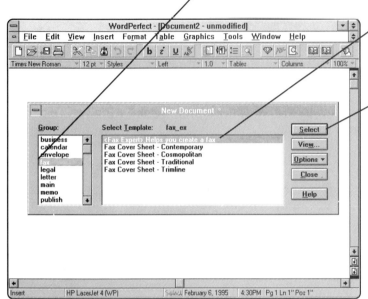

4. **Click** on **<Fax Expert>** in the Select Template list if it isn't already highlighted.

5. **Click** on **Select**. The dialog box will close. After a pause, a message asking you to "Please wait..." will appear. Finally, the Fax Expert opening dialog box will appear.

Selecting the Template Style

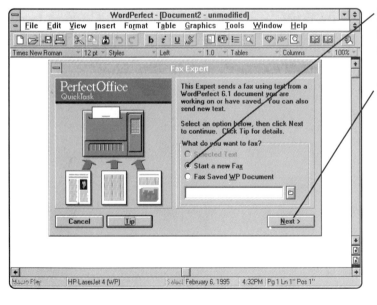

1. **Click** on **Start a New Fax** to place a dot in the circle if one is not already there.

2. **Click** on **Next**.

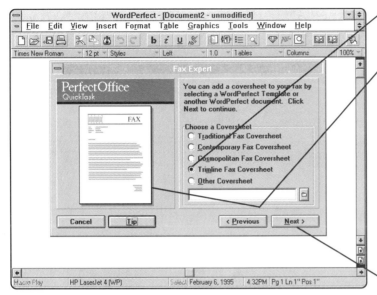

3. **Click** on **Trimline** to place a dot in the circle.

Notice that the Trimline style is shown in the preview box. Click on the other styles to preview them as well. If you want your screen to look like the examples in this chapter, be sure to click on Trimline once again before doing step 4.

4. **Click** on **Next**. After a pause, the Personalize Your Template dialog box will appear.

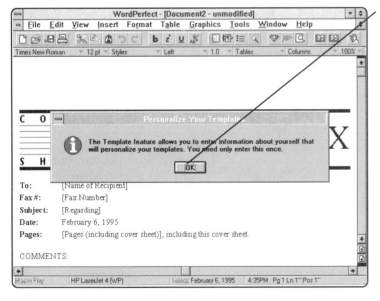

5. **Click** on **OK**. The dialog box will close. The Enter Your Personal Information dialog box will appear.

ENTERING YOUR PERSONAL INFORMATION

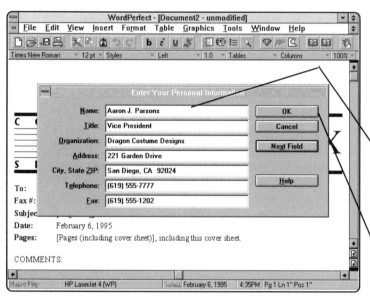

You have to enter your personal information only once. WordPerfect will keep this information on file and insert it automatically into future faxes.

1. **Type** your personal information. **Press Tab** to move through the text boxes.

2. **Click** on **OK**. The Template Information dialog box will appear.

CREATING AN ADDRESS BOOK

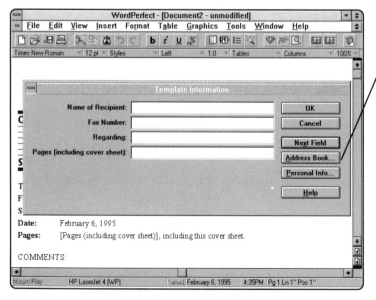

You can create an address book for frequent faxes.

1. **Click** on **Address Book**. The Template Address Book dialog box will open.

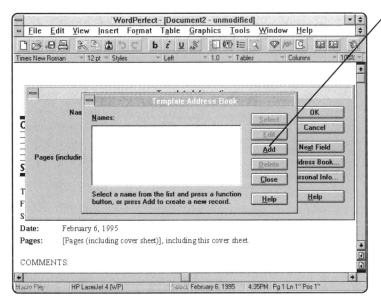

2. **Click** on **Add**. The Edit Address dialog box will appear.

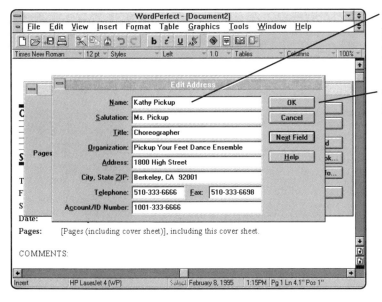

3. **Type** the information to be added to your Address Book.

4. **Click** on **OK**. The dialog box will close.

Notice that the name has been added to the Address Book list.

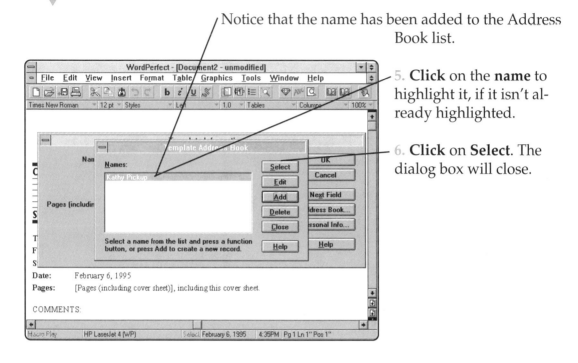

5. **Click** on the **name** to highlight it, if it isn't already highlighted.

6. **Click** on **Select**. The dialog box will close.

Notice that the name and fax number have been automatically inserted into the appropriate boxes in the Template Information dialog box.

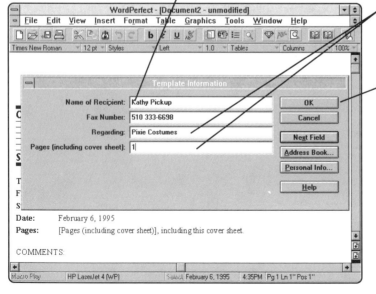

7. **Type** the appropriate "Regarding" and "Pages" information.

8 **Click** on **OK**. The dialog box will close. The Fax Expert dialog box will appear.

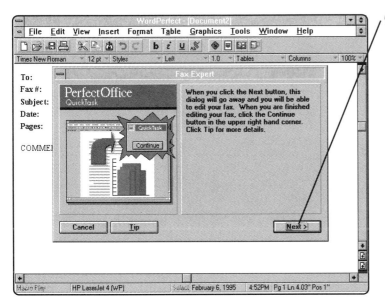

9. **Click** on **Next**.

10. **Type** any appropriate information to be included on the cover sheet.

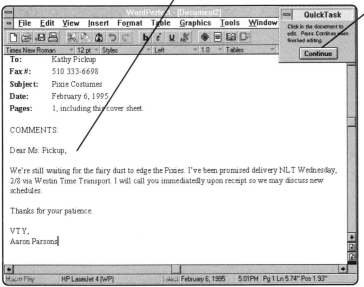

11. **Click** on **Continue**. The Fax Expert dialog box will reappear.

Notice the list of tasks that WordPerfect will automatically perform.

12. **Click** to insert an X in the box of any (or all) **tasks** that you want WordPerfect to perform at this time. In this example, we selected Spell Check, Save, and Print. This will give you a printed copy of the fax that you can send on your fax machine. If you have a fax program on your computer, click on Fax to send the fax through your computer.

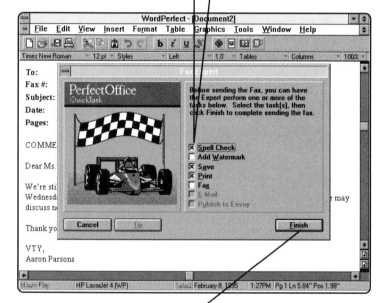

As soon as you close the Fax Expert dialog box, WordPerfect will bring up the appropriate dialog boxes to perform each of the tasks you have checked.

13. **Click** on **Finish**. The Fax Expert dialog box will close and the first of the tasks you've selected (if any) will begin.

If you need help with SpellCheck, please turn to Chapter 5, "Checking Grammar and Spelling, and Using the Thesaurus."

For help with Saving, please turn to Chapter 2, "Naming and Saving a Document."

If you need help with Printing, please turn to Chapter 3, "Printing a Document."

Installing
WordPerfect 6.1

This appendix walks you through a standard installation. If you want to customize your installation, refer to the *WordPerfect 6.1 for Windows Reference Manual*. In this appendix, you will do the following:

✔ Install WordPerfect
✔ Set up your printer to work with WordPerfect

INSTALLING WORDPERFECT 6.1 FOR WINDOWS

1. **Open** Windows by **typing win** at the DOS prompt (C:\>). The Program Manager opening screen will appear. Your screen may look different from this one.

Note: WordPerfect uses 11 disks to install the program. The first disk is labeled "Setup" and the rest are labeled "Program 1" through "Program 10."

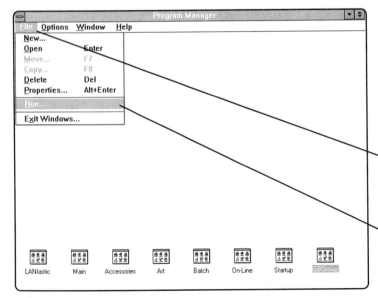

2. **Insert** the disk labeled "**Setup**" into drive A (or B). Put the disk into the slot with the metal piece going in first and the WordPerfect label face up.

3. **Click** on **File** in the menu bar. A pull-down menu will appear.

4. **Click** on **Run**. The Run dialog box will appear.

Notice that the cursor is flashing in the Command Line box. When you start typing, your text will be entered in the box.

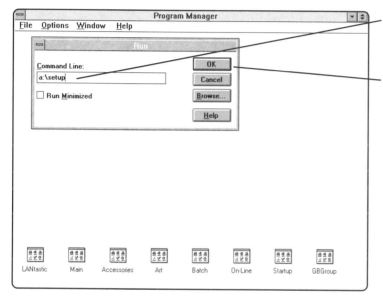

5. **Type a:\setup** (or b:\setup).

6. **Click** on **OK**. The WordPerfect 6.1 for Windows Setup dialog box will appear.

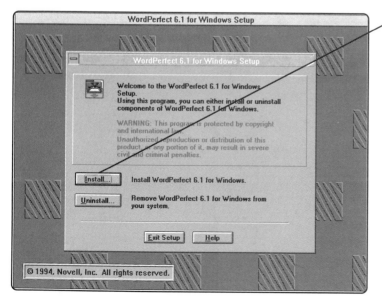

7. **Click** on **Install**. Next, the Registration Information dialog box will appear.

If you get an error message, it means you forgot to insert the disk.

Notice that the cursor is flashing in the Name box When you start typing, the cursor will disappear.

8. **Type** your **name** in the Name box and then **press Tab** to move the cursor to the Company name box.

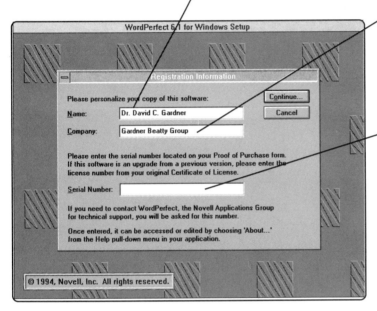

9. **Type** your **Company name,** if appropriate, and then **press Tab** to move the cursor to the Serial Number box.

10. **Type** in your **Serial Number** (or **license number** if you're installing an upgrade).

11. **Click** on **Continue.** The Installation Type dialog box will appear.

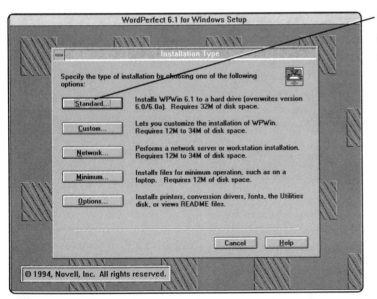

12. **Click** on **Standard**. After a pause the Select Drive dialog box will appear.

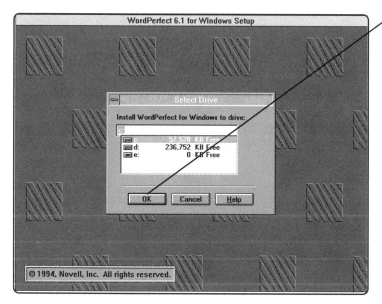

13. **Click** on **OK** since the C drive is already selected. (If you wish to install to another drive simply click on that drive and then on OK.)

At this point sit back and relax. Watch the background information and pictures change as WordPerfect copies the files from your disk to your hard drive. The Install Files dialog box will show you the percent of completion in copying files both for the disk you are currently copying, and as a percentage of all the disks.

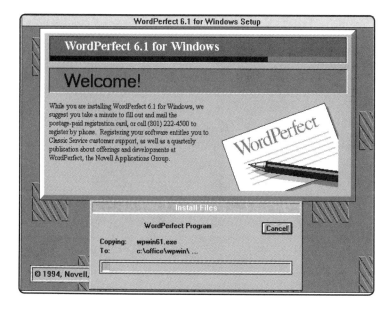

After WordPerfect is done copying the files from the Setup disk, the Diskette Needed dialog box will appear.

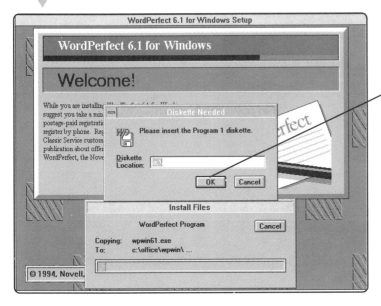

14. Remove the **Setup disk** from drive A (or B) and **insert** the **Program 1 disk**.

15. Click on **OK** or press Enter. The Diskette Needed dialog box will disappear. Word will begin copying the files on the Program 1 disk.

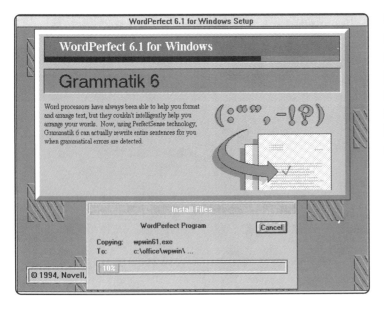

Once again the Install Files dialog box will appear and show you your percent of progress. WordPerfect will also continue to preview some of its features in the background while it is copying.

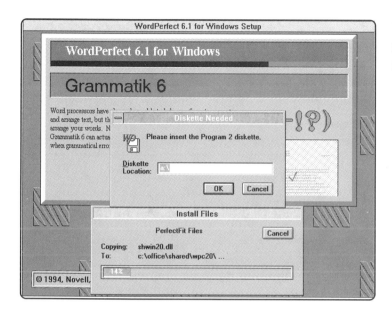

16. **Repeat steps 14 and 15** for the disks **Program 2 through Program 10**.

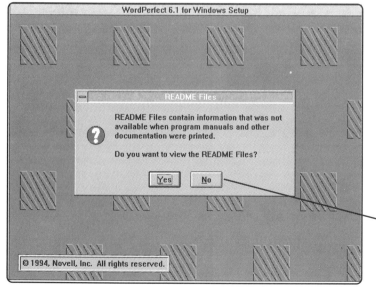

Towards the end of installing, you will see strange messages and things happening as WordPerfect busies itself with the final stages of the installation. Don't worry! This means you're almost done. Finally the ReadMe Files dialog box will appear.

17. **Click** on **No**. The "Installation Complete" dialog box will appear.

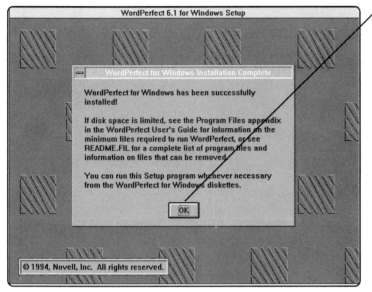

18. **Click** on **OK**. You will exit WordPerfect installation, and the program manager screen will reappear with your newly created WordPerfect 6.1 group.

Depending on your computer, you may get a message to exit Windows and reboot. When you've done this, you'll see the screen below.

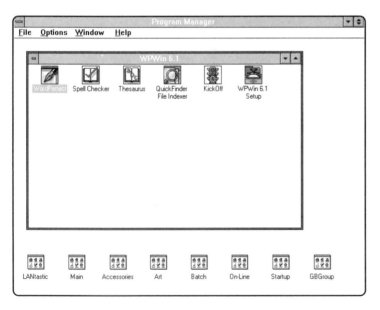

Congratulations! You have successfully installed WordPerfect.

Now you're ready to set up your printer to work with WordPerfect.

SETTING UP YOUR PRINTER TO WORK WITH WORDPERFECT

In this section, you'll set up your printer to work with WordPerfect by installing a *printer driver*, a special file that talks to your printer. We don't know why WordPerfect didn't give you the option of doing this during the main installation, but presumably they have their reasons.

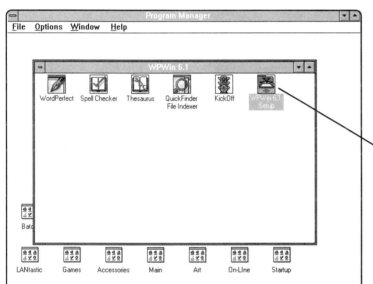

1. **Click twice** on the **WPWin6.1 Setup icon** in the WordPerfect group window. After a pause, the WordPerfect 6.1 for Windows Setup dialog box will appear (again).

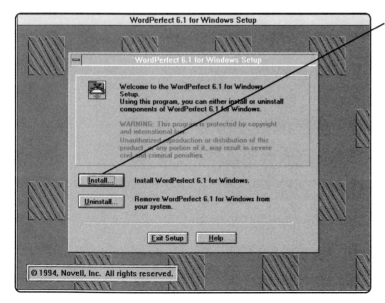

2. **Click** on **Install**. The Installation Type dialog box will appear (again).

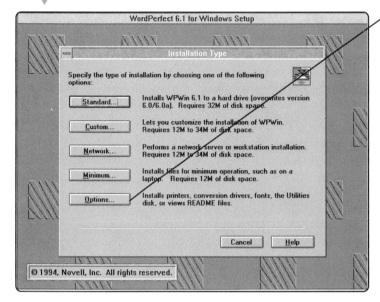

3. **Click** on **Options**. The Additional Installation Options dialog box will appear.

4. **Click** on **Printers**. The Select Printer Directory dialog box will appear.

5. **Insert** the WordPerfect 6.1 **Setup disk** in drive A (or B) once again.

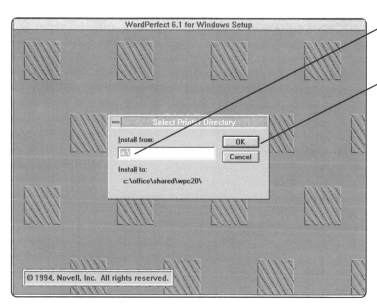

6. **Confirm** that the **correct drive** is highlighted.

7. **Click** on **OK**. After a pause, the WordPerfect Printer Drivers dialog box will appear. If you get a message saying, "Drive designator is invalid. Please retry," you didn't do step 5. Click on OK in the error message box, go back to step 5, and try again.

Selecting Your Printer

WordPerfect contains drivers for hundreds of different printers. In this section, you'll tell WordPerfect the name of your printer.

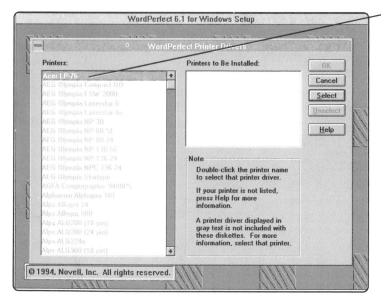

Notice that the first printer on the list is already high-lighted.

1. **Type** the **first letter** of your printer's name, for example, type the letter h if you have a Hewlett Packard printer. The highlight bar will move to the first printer beginning with the letter h. (This is much faster than scrolling through the entire list.)

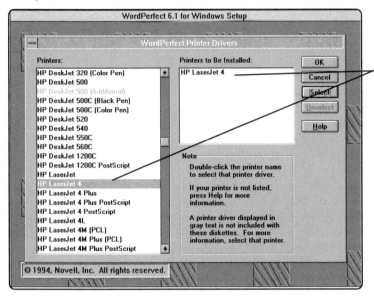

2. **Click** on the ↓ to scroll through the list of printers.

3. **Click twice** on the **name** of your printer. In this example, it is HP LaserJet 4. The name of your printer will appear in the Printers to Be Installed box.

4. **Click** on **OK**. After a pause, you'll see the message box below.

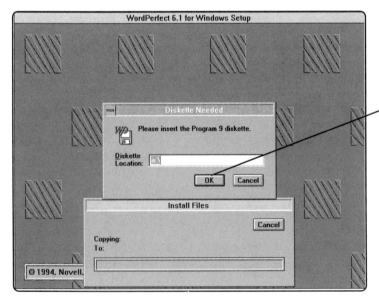

5. **Remove** the **Setup diskette** and **insert** the **Program 9 diskette** into Drive A (or B).

6. **Click** on **OK**. You'll see the (by now) familiar progress scale as your printer driver is installed.

When the installation is complete, you'll see the screen in the next example.

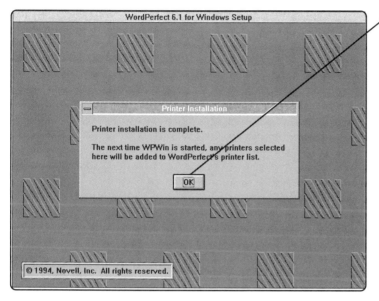

7. **Click** on **OK**. This dialog box will close, and the Additional Installation Options dialog box will be back on your screen.

From here you'll close a series of screens you've already seen.

8. **Click** on **Close**. The Installation Type dialog box will appear again.

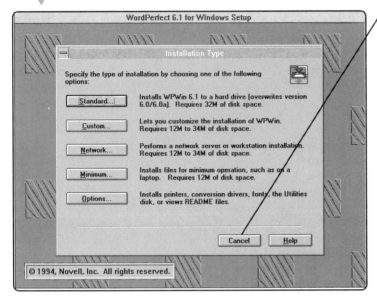

9. **Click** on **Cancel**. The WordPerfect 6.1 for Windows Setup box will appear again.

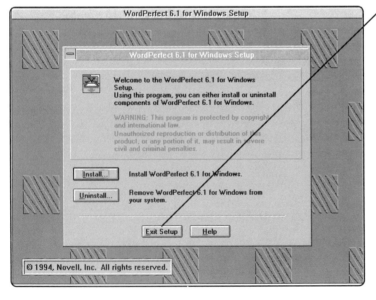

10. **Click** on **Exit Setup**. The WordPerfect group window will appear again.

At this point, you can go to Chapter 1, and have fun!

Note: Remember to remove the disk from drive A (or B).

Index

A

Abbreviations, 240-244
    creating entries, 240-243
    inserting abbreviations, 243-244
Absolute tabs, 105
Adding text, 44
Addresses. *see also* Form letters; Mailing lists;
        Return addresses
    Fax Expert, address book for, 250-254
    for letters, 11-12
Alignment of text, undoing, 72-73
Alphabetically sorting data in tables, 208-210
Arial font, 7
Automatic page break, 15

B

Bird's-eye view, 128-129
Boldfacing text, 66
Booting up WordPerfect, 29
Borders
    adding filled border, 91-94
    deleting borders, 94
Box symbols, 18-19
Bulleted lists, 74-75
    deleting bullets, 75
    tabs for, 100-102

C

Capitalizing text, 65
Case of text, conversion of, 65
Cells. *See* Tables
Center-aligned tabs
    defined, 99
    setting of, 114
Centering
    with Layout menu, 71

    with Power Bar, 69
    with QuickMenus, 70
    tables, 217-218
    undoing alignment, 72-73
Clip art. *See* Pictures
Closing
    after changes, 28
    files, 27-28
    labels file, 200
    open files, 142
    without saving, 119-120
    WordPerfect 6.1, 29
Colors in TextArt, 86-87
Columns. *See* Mailing lists; Tables
Combining paragraphs, 46-47
Copying
    form letters, copying field codes in, 169-171
    formulas, 223
    text, 57-59
C prompt, opening Windows from, 2-4
Currency format for numbers, 224-226
Cut button, deleting text with, 44-45

D

Data files
    for labels, 196-197
    mailing lists, 143-144
Dates on letters, 11-12
.dat file extension, 162
Decimal tabs
    defined, 99
    setting of, 115-116
Defaults
    for fonts, 6
    for margins, 5

NOTES

NOTES

NOTES